Santa's Hometown

How New York City*
Shaped the Christmas Season

*(and a few other places...)

Kevin Woyce

Copyright 2018 by Kevin Woyce

All Rights Reserved. No part of this book may be reproduced, stored, or transmitted, by any means, without the author's permission.

Author Photographs:
25. *Papier Mache Christmas Houses*
94. *Rockefeller Center Christmas Tree 2001*
95. *Radio City Music Hall*
96. *Rockefeller Center, Channel Gardens View*
97. *Saint Patrick's Cathedral*
107. *34th Street, photographed from Empire State*
110. *R.H. Macy & Company Main Entrance*
126. *Trinity Church*
152. *The Sun Building Clock*
155. *Mini Lights*

KevinWoyce.com

Contents

1.	The Night Before…	4
2.	Patron Saint of New York	10
3.	Knickerbocker's History	18
4.	Christmases Past	26
5.	The Portrait of Mr. Claus	44
6.	Reindeer Games	56
7.	O Christmas Tree	68
8.	Let There Be Lights	80
9.	Christmas at the Rock	92
10.	34th Street Miracles	106
11.	New Year, New York	120
12.	Christmas Unwrapped	134
	About the Author	156
	Bibliography	157

The Night Before...

On Christmas Eve, 1822, Clement Clarke Moore read a poem for his six young children. It began, "'Twas the night before Christmas."

A biblical scholar, Moore considered *A Visit from St. Nicholas* a "mere trifle." The work that had secured his professorship at the General Theological Seminary was a two-volume *Compendious Lexicon of the Hebrew Language*.

But Harriet Butler, a family friend, brought a handwritten copy of Moore's "trifle" home to Troy, New York, where her father was rector of St. Paul's Episcopal Church. She showed the copy to Reverend Butler, and then to Orville Holley, editor of the semiweekly *Troy Sentinel*. Holley published the poem in December 1823, without revealing the author's name.

Clement Clarke Moore

Holley reprinted *A Visit from St. Nicholas* every December until 1831, his last Christmas as editor. (The paper ceased publication the following year.) The closest he came to identifying Moore was in 1829, when he described the poet as "a scholar and writer" from "the City of New York." In 1830, Holley illustrated the verses with a woodcut by Troy engraver Myron King: Saint Nicholas flying over the rooftops in his reindeer-drawn sleigh.

Moore finally allowed *A Visit* to appear under his name in 1837, when *New York Mirror* editor Charles Fenno Hoffman included it in *The New-York Book of Poetry*. Hoffman also published three more serious poems by Moore. *From a Father to His Children, After Having Had his Portrait Taken for Them* begins:

This semblance of your parent's time-worn face
Is but a sad bequest, my children dear:
Its youth and freshness gone, and in their place
The lines of care, the tracks of many a tear!

In 1844, Clement Moore released a concisely-titled book: *Poems*. He had not planned to include *A Visit from St. Nicholas*, but his grown children talked him into it. Mary, who was just three years old the night he read about the "right jolly old elf," illustrated the first full-color edition of the *Visit* in 1855; she gave it as a gift to her husband, John Doughty Ogden. Nearly a century later, *Life* Magazine printed a facsimile of her 16-page booklet.

Clement Moore was born in 1779, the only child of Benjamin and Charity Moore. Bishop Benjamin Moore led the Episcopal Diocese of New York, and was twice president of Columbia College. Charity Clarke Moore inherited Chelsea, a Manhattan estate north of Houston Street. Her father, Major Thomas Clarke, had bought the property when he retired from the British Army after the French and Indian Wars. The main house, which Mary Moore Ogden sketched for her 1855 booklet, stood near the modern intersection of Ninth Avenue and 23rd Street.

Charity Moore gave the land to her son in 1813, when he married Catharine Taylor. The young couple moved their growing family into the old mansion in the early 1820s. Catharine bore nine children, seven of whom lived to adulthood. After she died in 1830, Clement Moore raised them alone; he never remarried.

Around the time Moore inherited Chelsea, the city announced plans to extend the street grid northward, driving Ninth Avenue through the estate. Moore tried to rally other landowners to fight these plans, but soon accepted the march of progress. He donated his apple orchard to Trinity Church in 1818, on the condition that the property be used for a Theological Seminary; the East Building opened there in 1827. Moore later gave lots for two churches: Saint Luke in the Fields, on Hudson Street between Christopher and Barrow; and Saint Peter's Episcopal Church, on the corner of Ninth Avenue and 20th Street. Because it was built of Manhattan schist, Saint Peter's is sometimes called "The Rock of Chelsea." Due to Moore's involvement, it is also known as "The Christmas Church."

Inset: 'Old Chelsea Mansion House' by Mary C. Ogden (1855)

With builder and property manager James Wells, Moore divided the rest of Chelsea into building lots. To maintain property values, they required buyers to sign covenants prohibiting the construction of stables, stores, and industrial buildings. In 1836, Moore moved his family into a brick townhouse on West 22nd Street. Though this house still stands, the original mansion was demolished when the city graded the new streets. The modern neighborhood of Chelsea, home to the High Line and more than 200 art galleries, stretches from the Hudson River to Sixth Avenue, between 14th Street and the upper 20's.

Many theories have been spun about the origin of Moore's best-known poem. In some accounts, he modeled "St. Nick" after a Dutch neighbor. A more elaborate story has him going to Greenwich Village on a snowy Christmas Eve to buy a turkey, because his wife was cooking Christmas dinners for the poor. On the way back, he dashed off the famous lines in a sleigh driven by a "lively and quick" old man with a white beard.

Or, the poem came to him in the early 1820s, while he was visiting his cousin, Mary Eliza Constable, in the Adirondacks. Mary's husband had died in May 1821, at the age of 35, leaving her with five young children and a 9,000 square foot stone mansion. All the windows in Constable Hall had shutters that opened on the inside, like the ones Moore described:

Away to the window I flew like a flash,
Tore open the shutters and threw up the sash

So Moore, who sent Mary a handwritten copy of the poem, may have modeled Saint Nicholas on the Constables' gardener, a plump Dutchman named Pieter. Though Constable Hall was restored as a museum in 1949, nobody knows what became of Moore's gift.

Another theory: Moore did not actually write *A Visit from Saint Nicholas*. Based on computer analysis of word choices and meter, some scholars believe the verses were composed by Henry Livingston, Jr. A distant relative of Moore's wife, Livingston died in 1828. He never claimed authorship, and there are no copies of the poem in his handwriting (The New York Historical Society owns one of four copies handwritten by Moore). But in 1899, one of Livingston's descendants published an article claiming that Henry first read the poem to his family and friends in 1807; the debate continues.

Patron Saint of New York

Manhattan has a St. Nicholas Avenue, running from 111th Street through Harlem and Washington Heights to 193rd. In Colonial times it was called Harlem Lane, or else Kingsbridge Road, after the first wooden bridge over the Harlem River.

There is also a St. Nicholas Terrace, which stretches from 127th to 140th, along the western edge of St. Nicholas Park. Named after the two streets, the wooded park was laid out in the 1890s, on a steep, rocky hillside; the main stairway, at 135th Street, has 135 steps. At the north end, visitors can tour Hamilton Grange National Monument. Alexander Hamilton had the house built in 1802, two years before his death. It was designed by John McComb, architect of Gracie Mansion and New York City Hall.

Saint Nicholas icon (c. 1294) – Lipnya Church of Saint Nicholas, Novgorod, Russia

The National Park Service began restoring Hamilton Grange in 2008, after moving it from its former location on Convent Avenue.

Saint Nicholas was probably born around 270 A.D. in Lycia, part of modern Turkey. After his wealthy parents died, he gave away all the money they left him and became a priest. While still a young man, he was appointed bishop of the Greek city of Myra (surviving ruins include a Roman theater and a hillside necropolis). Miracles attributed to him include bringing three murdered boys back to life and calming a storm during a sea voyage to the Holy Land.

The most popular story about Nicholas tells how he helped a man who had three daughters of marriageable age, but no money for their dowries. Three nights in a row, Nicholas walked past their home. Each night, he tossed a bag of gold coins through an open window. The bags landed in the girl's shoes, or in the stockings they washed every night and then hung by the fireplace to dry. In some accounts, their father waited up the last night and caught Nicholas at the window. The bishop asked the thankful man to keep his identity a secret.

After he died, Nicholas became a popular figure in both the Eastern Orthodox and Roman Catholic churches: the patron saint of children, sailors, and unwed maidens. Eastern icons show a slim, elderly man with a white beard, wearing red bishop's robes and holding a Bible. Roman artists added three coin purses, or three gold coins. Many pictures include children or ships.

Inset:
"Greetings from Saint Nicholas"
(Dutch greeting card, 19th century)

By the Middle Ages, Nicholas was a figure of legend, riding about the countryside on a large white horse and leaving coins in the shoes of the poor. People exchanged gifts on his feast day, December 6. (Like most saint's days, this was the anniversary of his death, not his birthday). In Belgium and the Netherlands, children set out snacks for *Sinterklaas*—and hay for his horse—on the evening of December 5. The following morning, they woke to find sweets, fruits, nuts, or other gifts in their shoes or stockings.

But in many places, *Sinterklaasfeest* was also celebrated like Mardi Gras, with costumes, masks, and rowdy drunken parades—basically, an old, pagan Winter Solstice festival with a new name. In England, the party broke out on Christmas Day, instead. Bands of carolers drunk on wassail (mulled wine) sang:

Bring us a figgy pudding and a cup of good cheer;
We won't go until we get some.

Or, in *The Wassail Song*:

Bring us out a table, and spread it with a cloth;
Bring us out a cheese, and of your Christmas loaf.

The Protestant Reformation began in Germany in 1517, when Martin Luther sent his *Ninety-Five Theses on the Power and Efficacy of Indulgences* to the Archbishop of Mainz. According to popular custom, Luther also nailed a copy of the document—a list of challenges inviting academic debate—to the door of All Saints' Church in his native Wittenberg.

Like most large movements, the Reformation soon split into factions, including the Lutherans (Germany), Anglicans (England), Presbyterians (Scotland), and the Reformed Churches of Switzerland and the Netherlands. These new churches did away with many of the traditions of Roman Catholicism in favor of a "priesthood of all believers." With Bibles translated into local languages, and mass produced on the new printing presses, people could finally read Scripture themselves. The new churches also taught them to speak directly to Heaven, rather than confessing to priests or praying for saints to intercede on their behalf. As a result, most Saints' Days—including *Sinterklaasfeest*—disappeared from Protestant calendars.

Henry VIII established the Church of England in 1534. Early in the 1600s, reformers sought to "purify" the Anglican Church of its old Roman Catholic influences, including choral and instrumental music. By 1640, more than 20,000 of these "Puritans" had crossed the Atlantic to settle New England.

Among the many things the Puritans disapproved of were Christmas Day celebrations. When Oliver Cromwell seized power in 1653, after the English Civil War, he outlawed the holiday, reserving the day for quiet reflection at home or in church. King Charles II brought back the rowdy merrymaking in the 1660s.

Following Cromwell's lead, the Boston government banned Christmas revelry in 1659. Though the law was repealed in 1681, the holiday went mostly unobserved in New England for another century and a half.

Some Reformers found a middle ground. German Protestants moved the gift-giving holiday from December 6 to Christmas Day. Instead of Saint Nicholas, children waited all year for the *Christkindl*—"Christ Child"—to fill their stockings with toys or treats. In some accounts, Martin Luther invented the angelic visitor to encourage children to mind their manners and say their prayers throughout the year. Over time, *Christkindl* became the secular "Kris Kringle."

Inset: Vintage European *Christkindl* card

The Dutch Reformed churches stamped out the wilder aspects of *Sinterklaasfeest*, but families continued to honor the old bishop in their homes. Children still left him snacks at night and found gifts in the morning. In some versions of his legends, *Sinterklaas* had magical assistants who told him which children had been good in the past year, and which had not.

When the Dutch settled Manhattan and the Hudson River Valley in the 1620s, they brought Saint Nicholas with them. The Saint Nicholas Collegiate Reformed Protestant Dutch Church began holding services in a grist mill in 1628. Five years later, Reverend Everardus Bogardus moved the congregation into New Amsterdam's first real church. The small wooden building was enlarged and rebuilt of stone in 1642.

The church moved one last time in 1872, to the corner of Fifth Avenue and 48th Street. Theodore Roosevelt worshipped at the impressive brownstone building when he was in New York, and his memorial service took place there on January 30, 1919. But the congregation sold the property in 1949, for the expansion of Rockefeller Center; the corner is now occupied by the 28-story Sinclair Oil Building.

The *New-York Gazette* reported in December 1773 that some of the city's Dutch families still celebrated the annual feast of "St. A. Claus." But the Dutch were no longer the majority in New York, and newer arrivals brought their own traditions. It would be another 30 years before the New York Historical Society nominated Nicholas as the city's patron saint. They also adopted the Bishop of Myra as the Society's patron, and popularized the tradition of giving Christmas gifts in his name.

Knickerbocker's History

The *New York Evening Post* printed the first notice on October 26, 1809. "A small elderly gentleman ... by the name of Knickerbocker" had been missing for several weeks from the Colombian Hotel on Mulberry Street. "As there are some reasons for believing he is not entirely in his right mind," the landlord asked readers to report any sightings.

A second notice appeared three weeks later. The hotel owner, who identified himself as Seth Handaside, thanked the paper for publishing the first ad. He then explained that "a very curious kind of a written book has been found in his room," and that he would be forced to publish it if Knickerbocker did not return to pay his bill. On November 28, Handaside said the book would be released the following Wednesday: December 6.

And so it was:

A History of New York,
from the Beginning of the World to the End of the Dutch Dynasty;

Containing, among many surprising and curious matters, the unutterable ponderings of Walter the Doubter, the Disastrous Projects of William the Testy, and the Chivalric Achievements of Peter the Headstrong; the three Dutch Governors of New Amsterdam; Being the only authentic history of the times that ever hath been or ever will be published.

New Yorkers soon learned that old Knickerbocker had never been missing, nor had he owed any money to Seth Handaside. Both men were figments of the real author's imagination, but they served their purpose well. Washington Irving's first book was an immediate success, and he put out revised editions in 1812, 1819, and 1848. In these editions, Irving explained how the whole two-volume "history" began as a simple parody of a pretentious New York City guidebook.

Washington Irving was born in the city in 1783, the last of William and Sarah Irving's eleven children (eight survived to adulthood). When he was six years old, he met the man his parents named him after: George Washington. They never saw each other again, but Irving spent his last years writing a five-volume biography of the first president.

New York in summer was hot and crowded. Epidemics were common. When yellow fever hit the city in 1798, Irving's parents sent him to stay with relatives in nearby Tarrytown. While there, the teenager became fascinated by Dutch folktales and ghost stories.

Irving began writing professionally four years later. Between November 1802 and April 1803, the *Morning Chronicle* published nine letters mocking New York fashion, manners, and theater critics. All were signed "Jonathan Oldstyle," but Irving's identity was no secret. (His brother Peter edited the *Chronicle*, which was partly owned by Aaron Burr.)

With his brother William, and their friend James Paulding, Irving launched his own periodical in January, 1807. Like the Oldstyle letters, *Salmagundi* satirized New York City life. Washington did most of the writing under a variety of pseudonyms, including Launcelot Langstaff, Will Wizard, and Mustapha Khan.

Salmagundi ran only 20 issues, the last released on January 15, 1808. In the November 1807 issue, Irving gave New York one of its most enduring nicknames: **Gotham**.

He borrowed the name from a village in Nottinghamshire, England. According to a medieval folktale, the people of Gotham once pretended to be lunatics or fools. They were so convincing, the king decided to reroute a trip rather than visit the place!

Washington Irving

"Gotham," Irving assured his readers,

is most shockingly ill-natured and sarcastic, and wickedly given to all manner of backslidings; for which we are very sorry, indeed.

The Joker would approve. Bill Finger and Bob Kane introduced "The Bat-Man" in the May 1939 *Detective Comics*. Neither could decide what to call their Caped Crusader's hometown until the following year, when Finger spotted a "Gotham Jewelers" in a New York phonebook.

Irving's *History of New York* had an even bigger influence on popular culture.

Manhattanites—especially those with a real or imagined connection to the early Dutch settlers—began calling themselves "Knickerbockers" after his eccentric narrator. In the 1840s, bank clerk Alexander Cartwright joined the city's Knickerbocker Engine Company No. 12 as a volunteer fireman. In his spare time, he and his friends played a new game known variously as "town ball," "round ball," or—in New York—"base ball."

By 1845, Cartwright had assembled a team of players, which he called the "New York Knickerbockers" after the Engine Company. They played their first official game the following year at Hoboken's Elysian Fields, losing to the "New York Nine." Besides forming the team, Cartwright is credited with writing down one of the first lists of instructions for the game—known, of course, as "The Knickerbocker Rules."

The baseball Knickerbockers disbanded in the 1870s. Promoter Ned Irish revived the name for the city's first pro basketball franchise in 1946. The

"Knicks" played their first game that November, beating the Toronto Huskies: 68-66.

An early London edition of Irving's *History* included humorous drawings by George Cruikshank, who also illustrated the first edition of Charles Dickens's *Oliver Twist*. Cruickshank dressed Irving's portly Dutchmen in baggy trousers, cinched at the knee. When similar pants came back into fashion in the 1860s, people called them "knickerbockers."

Throughout the *History*, Irving exaggerated the role Saint Nicholas played in Dutch culture. He said the first settlers crossed the Atlantic in "a mighty ark ... under the protection of St. Nicholas." The ship's figurehead was "a goodly image of St. Nicholas." But Irving's Nicholas had more in common with a prosperous Dutch businessman than the bishop of Myra, with his

low, broad-brimmed hat, a huge pair of Flemish trunk-hose, and a pipe that reached to the end of the bowsprit.

In one chapter, Irving promised to explain:

How the city of New Amsterdam waxed great under the protection of St. Nicholas and the absence of laws and statutes.

In another, Director-General Peter ("The Headstrong") Stuyvesant *swore by the pipe of St. Nicholas, which like the sacred fire, was never extinguished.*

Irving also described how Dutch families performed the "pious ceremony"

... of hanging up a stocking in the chimney on St. Nicholas eve; which stocking is always found in the morning miraculously filled.

For the 1812 edition, Irving inserted the dream of one Olaf van Kortlandt:

...the good St. Nicholas came riding over the tops of the trees, in that self-same wagon wherein he brings his yearly presents to children...

Ten years later, Clement Moore substituted a "sleigh full of toys" for the wagon, and fleshed out Irving's description of a Nicholas who "looked like a peddler just opening his pack," with

*a broad face and a little round belly
that shook when he laughed,
like a bowl full of jelly.*

More significantly for children and retailers, Moore changed the date of the old man's arrival, from December fifth to "the night before Christmas."

Papier Mache Christmas Houses
Decorated and photographed by the author

Christmases Past

Washington Irving sailed to England in 1815. He planned to spend just a few months, helping his older brothers rebuild their importing business, which had collapsed during the War of 1812. Though the business soon failed, Washington remained overseas until May, 1832.

While in London, Irving befriended the Scottish poet Walter Scott, who had recently begun publishing a series of popular historical novels. *Waverly* was the first, in 1814; *Rob Roy* followed in 1817, *Ivanhoe* in 1819. Because novels were not yet considered serious literature, Scott published them anonymously until 1827; most were attributed only to "The Author of Waverly." But during their conversations and correspondence, Scott encouraged Irving to resume his own writing career, which had stalled after the publication of his *History of New York*.

By the spring of 1819, Irving had written 29 short stories and essays. He mailed them to his brother Ebenezer a few at a time, for serial publication as *The Sketch Book of Geoffrey Crayon, Gent*. New York publisher C.S. Van Winkle released the first installment on June 23, 1819. Four of the five pieces, including *The Author's Account of Himself*, were attributed to Crayon; Diedrich Knickerbocker got credit for the last, *Rip Van Winkle*. Three more installments appeared that year, on July 31, September 13, and November 10. All were printed simultaneously in New York, Baltimore, Boston, and Philadelphia.

Five Christmas sketches filled the next issue, which landed on January 1, 1820. Irving's narrator explained:

Nothing in England exercises a more delightful spell over my imagination than the lingerings of the holiday customs and rural games of former times.

In the second sketch, Crayon described a Christmas Eve stage coach ride "to the family mansion of the Bracebridges." Though all the characters he meets are figments of Irving's imagination, the mansion was real. Irving lived for a while in Birmingham with his sister Sarah and her husband, Henry van Wart.

'Christmas Day,' by Randolph Caldecott
From an 1899 edition of Irving's Christmas sketches

Born in Tarrytown, New York, van Wart had moved to England to run the Liverpool branch of the Irving family business. When that failed, he took his family to Birmingham and set up his own company to ship the city's products to the United States.

While in Birmingham, Irving attended a Christmas celebration at Aston Hall. Now one of the city's most popular museums, Aston Hall was built between 1618 and 1635 for Sir Thomas Holte.

Aston Hall, Birmingham

The mansion remained in the baronet's family until 1818, when it was leased to James Watt, Jr., son of the steam engine pioneer. In his sketches, Irving renamed the place "Bracebridge Hall" after Mary Elizabeth Bracebridge, the last Holte descendant to live there.

On Christmas Eve, Crayon found the house filled with several generations of Bracebridge family and friends. Along with dancing, dining, and singing,

The Yule clog[1] and Christmas candle were regularly burnt, and the mistletoe with its white berries hung up, to the imminent peril of all the pretty housemaids.

He was awakened Christmas morning by children singing carols outside his door. After breakfast, he accompanied the family to church for "a most erudite sermon on the rites and ceremonies of Christmas." This stretched into a history lesson, as the parson described how

> *the Puritans made such a fierce assault upon the ceremonies of the Church, and poor old Christmas was driven out of the land by proclamation of Parliament.*

Irving's final Christmas sketch described dinner at Bracebridge Hall, where "The table was literally loaded with good cheer, and presented an epitome of country abundance," including "a pie magnificently decorated with peacock's feathers."

The final two installments of the *Sketch Book* were published in March and September, 1820. *The Legend of Sleepy Hollow*, attributed to Diedrich Knickerbocker, closed the March issue.

In England, Irving published the entire *Sketch Book* in two hardcover volumes, the first in February 1820, the second in July. Modern printings include 34 sketches: the 29 that appeared in the American periodical, three that Irving added to the British edition, and two that he wrote for an 1848 reprint.

Irving spent most of the 1820s exploring Europe. At various times he lived in Dresden, Paris, and Madrid. While in Spain, he wrote three books based on the life of Christopher Columbus, freely mixing history and fiction; his most notorious invention is the idea that fifteenth century Europeans believed the world was flat, until Columbus proved them wrong.

After returning to the United States in the spring of 1832, Irving spent several years exploring the West. Along the way, he wrote *A Tour of the Prairies*; a book about John Jacob Astor's Pacific Fur Company; and a biography of western explorer Benjamin Bonneville. He finally settled down in 1835, at an estate south of Tarrytown that he named "Sunnyside" in 1841.

The literary sensation of 1841 was Charles Dickens's fourth novel, *The Old Curiosity Shop*. "Very interesting," Queen Victoria called it, "and cleverly written." Like most of Dickens's novels, it first appeared as a serial, in 88 weekly installments published between April 1840 and November 1841. When the last part was due, New Yorkers waited at the docks to learn the fate of their heroine, "Little Nell" Trent.

On January 3, 1842, Dickens left Liverpool aboard the wooden-hulled, sidewheel passenger steamer *RMS Britannia*. Nineteen days later, he stepped ashore in Boston. "The city is a beautiful one," he wrote, "and cannot fail ... to impress all strangers."

By February 1, Dickens was in New York, where Washington Irving hosted a dinner for him. The two authors, who admired each other's work, had recently struck up an overseas correspondence.

Dickens told the crowd that he did not "go to bed two nights out of seven without taking Washington Irving under my arm upstairs to bed with me." Writing to a London friend, Dickens said, "Washington Irving is a great fellow. We have laughed most heartily together." Later in the month, Irving entertained Dickens and his wife at Sunnyside.

The two met one last time in the spring of 1842 at the White House, where President John Tyler appointed Irving United States Minister to Spain. "As long as I live," Dickens wrote, "I shall never forget the privilege of my association with you."

Irving's *Sketch Book* inspired the Christmas scenes in the Dickens's first novel, *The Pickwick Papers*, which was published between March 1836 and October 1837. Chapter 28 is subtitled *A good-humoured Christmas Chapter, containing an Account of a Wedding, and some other Sports beside*. On Christmas Eve, "a huge branch of mistletoe" unleashes a "scene of general and most delightful struggling and confusion."

There were no country Christmases in Dickens' own childhood. He was twelve years old in 1824, when his father was jailed for failing to pay a debt. Charles had to leave school to work ten hour days in a boot blacking factory. Every morning and evening, he visited his father at the notorious Marshalsea debtor's prison; thirty years later, he poured his still-vivid memories of the place into *Little Dorrit*.

Mistletoe scene from *The Pickwick Papers*
Drawing by 'Phiz' (Hablot K. Browne), 1874

Dickens spent five months touring the eastern United States and Canada, before returning to England in June, 1842. The trip was not a success. In October, he published a critical account of his travels, *American Notes for General Circulation*.

The United States, he wrote, was "not the republic of my imagination."

I was quite oppressed by the prevailing seriousness and melancholy air of business; which was so general and unvarying, that at every new town I came to, I seemed to meet the very same people whom I had left behind me.

The fact that slavery still existed sickened him; so did the filth of the major cities.

In America, Dickens had been welcomed like a latter-day rock star. "If I turn into the street," he wrote in a letter, "I am followed by a multitude." With the publication of *American Notes*, the multitude felt betrayed. Even in England, readers were put off by his bitterness. Critics called the book "boring."

That December, Dickens launched a new monthly serial, *The Life and Adventures of Martin Chuzzlewit*. For the first and only time, he sent some of his characters to the United States, where they were cheated by conmen.

By the fall of 1843, Dickens was having money troubles. His wife was pregnant with their fifth child. *Martin Chuzzlewit* was selling poorly, about a third as many copies each month as *The Old Curiosity Shop* had just two years before. During his long nighttime walks through London, Dickens worked out a new story, inspired by fairy tales and by Irving's sketches of English country Christmases, but also informed by his recent visit to a school for the poor.

He began writing the book in October and completed it in just six weeks. Instead of serializing it like his longer works, he decided to publish immediately in hardcover. *Punch* cartoonist John Leech drew the illustrations: four black and white woodcuts, and four etchings that had to be hand-colored. (These proved so costly that Dickens never again published a book with color pictures.)

'Mr. Fezziwig's Ball,' by John Leech, frontispiece for the 1843 first edition *of A Christmas Carol*

Due to *Chuzzlewit*'s slow sales, Dickens agreed to pay the production costs for his new work, in return for a share of the profits. *A Christmas Carol in Prose, Being a Ghost Story of Christmas* hit stores on December 19. With gilt-edged pages bound in red cloth, the slim volume sold for five shillings (about $30 in 2018), but the entire 6,000-copy first printing sold out by Christmas Eve. Chapman and Hall put out two more editions before the end of the year, and another ten in 1844.

By 1848, Dickens had written four more Christmas novellas, including *The Chimes* (1844) and *The Cricket on the Hearth* (1845). During these same years, he also wrote *The Life of Our Lord*, a short biography of Jesus which he read to his children each Christmas; in accordance with his wishes, it was not published until 1934, after the last of his children died.

Dickens gave his first public reading of *A Christmas Carol* on December 27, 1852, at the Birmingham Town Hall. In his later years, he became as famous for these dramatic readings—he acted out all the parts—as he was for his books. He started his first tour of the United Kingdom in April 1858. By February 1859, he had given 129 readings in 49 cities.

Scrooge and Marley's Ghost, drawn by John Leech for the 1843 first edition of *A Christmas Carol*

After a second UK tour in 1866, Dickens returned to the United States in November, 1867. Once again he landed in Boston, where he dined with famous writers, including Longfellow and Emerson (his old correspondent, Irving, had died in 1859). From December through April he did 76 readings, 22 of them at New York's Steinway Hall on East 14th Street. The readings were well attended; thanks to the increasing popularity of *A Christmas Carol*, the American public had mostly forgiven—or forgotten—his *American Notes*.

On April 18, 1868, the editors of the nation's biggest newspapers held a dinner for Dickens at Delmonico's Restaurant. Dickens spoke of the changes he had witnessed during his travels, adding:

Nor am I, believe me, so arrogant as to suppose that in five-and-twenty years there have been no changes in me, and that I had nothing to learn and no extreme impressions to correct when I was here first.

According to the *New York Tribune*:

Dickens' second coming was needed to disperse every cloud and every doubt, and to place his name undimmed in the silver sunshine of American admiration.

Charles Dickens reading (1870)

In all later editions of *American Notes* and *Martin Chuzzlewit*, Dickens included an excerpt from his Delmonico's speech, thanking his American readers for their "unsurpassable politeness, delicacy, sweet temper, hospitality, consideration, and ... unsurpassable respect."

Dickens made one last tour of the UK in 1868 and '69, and a final series of readings at London's

St. James's Hall in the first months of 1870; he died that June of a stroke. His most popular subjects were an abridged *Christmas Carol*, which he performed 127 times, and a trial scene from *The Pickwick Papers*; sometimes, he substituted one of the other Christmas stories for the *Carol*.

By February 1844, there were three theatrical adaptations of *A Christmas Carol* running in London. Dozens more followed. The first film version, *Scrooge, Or Marley's Ghost*, debuted in November 1901. Directed by British stage magician Walter Booth, the eleven minute silent presented the story in twelve brief scenes introduced by title cards. "Scene II. **Marley's Ghost** Shows Scrooge Visions of himself in CHRISTMASSES PAST." (As in some of the early theater productions, Marley is the film's only spirit, standing in for the Ghosts of Christmases Past, Present, and Yet-To-Come.) Less than half of the film survives. Though the acting and sets look amateurish today, the ghostly effects—Marley is semi-transparent—were state of the art in 1901.

MGM produced the classic black-and-white *A Christmas Carol* in 1938, starring Reginald Owen as Ebenezer Scrooge; CBS aired the British television version with George C. Scott in 1984. The Walt Disney Company has released two children's adaptations: *Mickey's Christmas Carol* in 1983 and *The Muppet Christmas Carol*, starring Michael Caine as Scrooge, in 1992.

Carol Brothers carol, carol joyfully,
Carol for the coming of Christ's Nativity.

Carolers, from a 1910 Christmas card

Oxford defines a **carol** as "a religious folk song or popular hymn, particularly one associated with Christmas." The word originated in France, where Christmas carols are also called *Noels*. Many early carols were written by medieval troubadours, who fit new words to old folk melodies. During the Protestant Reformation, clergy—including Martin Luther—began composing scripturally accurate songs, which they incorporated into Christmas services.

In the early 1800s, two books reintroduced caroling to England. Davies Gilbert compiled the first, *Some Ancient Christmas Carols, With the Tunes to Which They Were Formerly Sung in the West of England*, in 1822. A decade later, lawyer William Sandys published *Christmas Carols, Ancient and Modern*. Most of the 80 lyrics are presented without music, but the 18 melodies on the last pages include *I Saw Three Ships*, *The First Nowell*,[2] and *God Rest Ye Merry, Gentlemen*.

Many of today's most popular carols were composed, translated, or adapted in the nineteenth century; *Silent Night* in 1818, *O Come All Ye Faithful* and *It Came Upon a Midnight Clear* in the 1840s, and *Good King Wenceslas* in 1853. (Wenceslas was a tenth century Bohemian Duke who gave his subjects gifts of food, firewood, or clothing every Christmas.) *Angels We Have Heard on High* was adapted from a French carol in 1862; the decade also gave us *O Little Town of Bethlehem* and *We Three Kings of Orient Are*. *Away in a Manager* was written in 1885.

Antique advertising card (detail)

Christmas card from 1914

In keeping with musical tradition, Dickens called the chapters of his *Christmas Carol in Prose* "staves." The first four are identified with the arrivals of Jacob Marley and the three Christmas Ghosts; the last, in which the old miser wakes up a changed man, is simply titled *The End of It*.

[1] "Yule Clog" is one of several contemporary variations on the more popular "Yule Log."

[2] An early English spelling of the French "Noel."

The Portrait of Mr. Claus

A year before Moore introduced *A Visit from St. Nicholas*, his neighbor William Gilley published *The Children's Friend*. Subtitled *A New-Year's Present to the Little Ones from Five to Twelve*, the 16-page booklet included a Christmas poem by preacher Arthur Stansbury and eight hand-colored lithographs by William Barnet and Isaac Doolittle. It sold for 25 cents (about six dollars in 2018).

Moore probably read the book. Stansbury was a fellow Columbia graduate. Gilley published the *Episcopal Psalter* and the *Book of Common Prayer*. Like Moore, Stansbury had "Old Santeclaus" fly "o'er chimney tops, and tracks of snow … Each Christmas eve." He may also have been the first writer to substitute a reindeer (yes, just one) for Nicholas's white horse.

'Santeclaus' from *The Children's Friend* (1821)
Lithograph by William Barnet and Isaac Doolittle

Stansbury's Santeclaus is a less appealing character than Irving's or Moore's Nicholas. To "good girls or boys, that hated quarrels, strife and noise," he brought carefully selected toys and books. "But where I found the children naughty ... I left a long, black birchen rod."

Still, *The Children's Friend* contains some of the earliest known drawings of Santa Claus. In one, he occupies a sleigh hitched to a reindeer. (Keeping with the moralizing tone of the poem, the sleigh is decorated with the word "Rewards.) This Santa resembles a bearded garden gnome wearing a Russian fur hat. On another page, he looks more like the historical Saint Nicholas, an elderly, white-bearded man in a long red coat and hat.

Thomas Nast was born in 1840, in the German town of Landau. His mother brought him to New York in 1846. His father, a trombonist in a Bavarian military band, arrived four years later, after his enlistment ended; in New York, he supported his family by playing in theater orchestras.

The younger Nast left school at fourteen, to study drawing at the National Academy of Design. He began drawing professionally in 1856 for one of the city's popular new weeklies, *Frank Leslie's Illustrated Newspaper*.

English publisher Herbert Ingram had launched the *Illustrated London News* on May 14, 1842. The first 16-page issue, with 32 woodcut pictures and articles about Queen Victoria's first masquerade ball, a French train crash, and the ongoing war in Afghanistan, sold 26,000 copies. By 1851, the paper was selling 150,000 copies a week and had dozens of imitators.

Henry Carter left his father's prosperous glove making business in the 1840s to study wood engraving. He moved from England to New York in 1848, adopted the pen name "Frank Leslie," and opened an engraving shop on Broadway. Showman P.T. Barnum gave him his first big break, commissioning a program for "Swedish Nightingale" Jenny Lind's 1849 New York debut. Leslie also printed the programs for Lind's national tours in 1850 and 1851.

When Barnum began publishing *The Illustrated News* in 1853, Leslie made the engravings. The *News* lasted less than a year, but inspired Leslie to launch two periodicals of his own: *Frank Leslie's Ladies' Gazette of Fashion* and *Frank Leslie's Journal of Romance* (an illustrated fiction magazine). Both sold well enough that he was able to launch his weekly newspaper in 1855. Circulation exploded during the Civil War. By the 1870s, he had 300 employees, including 70 artists. Though Leslie died in 1880, the *Illustrated Newspaper* survived until 1922.

John and James Harper started a New York publishing company in 1817. Their younger brothers, Joseph and Fletcher, joined a few years later. By 1825, Harper & Brothers was the nation's largest book publisher.

Fletcher Harper published the first issue of *Harper's Magazine* in 1850. The monthly sold so well that he launched the illustrated *Harper's Weekly*—subtitled "A Journal of Civilization"—in 1857. By 1860, the circulation topped 200,000.

Thomas Nast sold his first cartoon to *Harper's* in 1859. Three years later, Fletcher hired him as a staff artist. Over the next 24 years, *Harper's*

Weekly published more than 2,200 Nash drawings; the last appeared in December, 1886.

Many of these drawings were political cartoons. *Harper's* supported President Lincoln and the Union Army during the Civil War, and the Republican Party for decades after. After Grant won the 1868 election, he thanked "the sword of Sheridan and the pencil of Thomas Nast."

Nast's loyalty did, however, have limits. When he felt the party was stumbling in the 1874 elections, he portrayed "The Republican Vote" as a confused elephant. (It would take another decade for the GOP to adopt the beast for a mascot.)

In the late 1860s, Nast turned his pencil against Tammany Hall, the corrupt Democratic political machine that practically ran New York City. He often depicted Tammany as a devouring tiger, and once drew "The Brains" of the machine—"Boss" William Tweed—with a moneybag for a head.

Tweed feared the popular cartoons so much that he offered to pay Nast $100,000 to stop drawing them. Nast pretended to negotiate until the bribe reached half a million, and then announced his intention to "put some of those fellows behind the bars." Tweed was finally driven from power after the November 1871 elections. Two years later, he was arrested for fraud.

'Christmas Eve' by Thomas Nast (1862)

Merciless as Nast could be—he once said, "I try to hit the enemy between the eyes and knock him down"—he also had a sentimental side. *Harper's* printed the first of his many Christmas drawings in 1862. Two wreaths framed Christmas Eve scenes: one of a Union soldier looking at pictures of his family by firelight, the other of his wife praying while their children slept.

Nast drew his first Santa Claus the following December. Dressed like Uncle Sam in striped trousers and a coat covered with stars, the jolly old man is giving out gifts at a Union Army camp. The soldiers laugh and cheer as he shows off a dancing puppet of Confederate President Jefferson Davis. The picture was so popular, Lincoln called Nast "our best recruiting sergeant."

Over the next 20 years, Nast refined his image of Santa. For 1866, he prepared an elaborate spread with multiple insets, *Santa Claus and His Works*. Like Moore, he presented Santa as an "elf," so small he had to stand on a chair to reach the stockings on the fireplace mantel. But Nast also added to the legend, drawing Santa making clothes for dolls, decorating a tree, and relaxing at his cozy home in "Santaclausville." *Harper's* ran the picture in black and white. When a full-color version appeared in an 1869 edition of Moore's *Visit*, Santa's fur-trimmed suit was revealed to be bright red; from then on, Claus was rarely depicted in other colors.

In 1871, Nast drew Santa at his desk, reading his mail. There is a towering stack of "Letters from Naughty Children's Parents" on one side, a much smaller pile of "Letters from Good Children's Parents" on the other. By 1884, he had Santa answering children's phone calls.

Inset: Santa Claus, by Thomas Nast (1881)

Santa Reading his Mail, by Thomas Nast (1871)

Nast drew his most popular Santa in 1881—round and bearded with a full white beard, a red suit, and a sack of toys on his back. Except for his long, smoking pipe—a detail borrowed from Irving and Moore—he looks much the way we picture him today.

Harper & Brothers released a slim book in 1890, *Thomas Nast's Christmas Drawings for the Human Race.* The pictures are identified by name in the "Stocking of Contents," under a sketch of a miniature Santa popping out of a stocking like a Christmas puppy.

Like Thomas Nast, Norman Rockwell began selling his art while still in his teens. Born on New York's Upper West Side in 1894, he enrolled in Chase Art School at fourteen. He also took classes at the National Academy of Design and at the Art Students League, where he learned figure drawing from George Bridgman, the author of *Constructive Anatomy.* Rockwell's first clients included *Boys' Life* and other "youth magazines."

George Barton, one of the founders of the American Boy Scouts, published the first eight-page issue of *Boys' and Boy Scouts' Magazine* in January, 1911. He shortened the title to *Boys' Life* for the 48-page March issue, and then sold the magazine to the rival Boy Scouts of America in 1912. The BSA published its first issue that July.

The editors of *Boys' Life* hired Norman Rockwell as a staff artist in 1912. When he turned nineteen the following year, they promoted him to Art Director, for a monthly salary of $50. He painted four covers that year, including the first of his many Christmas pictures: *Santa and Scouts in Snow*—a humorous scene of two boy scouts helping a clumsy Santa out of a snow bank.

Rockwell left the city for the suburban art colony of New Rochelle in 1914. He shared his first studio there with Clyde Forsyth, a western painter who often drew cartoons for the weekly *Saturday Evening Post*. Encouraged by Forsyth, Rockwell sold his first cover to the *Post* in May, 1916. By the end of the year, longtime editor George Horace Lorimer had bought seven more, including a Christmas painting, and Rockwell had left his job at *Boys' Life*.

Between 1916 and 1963, the *Saturday Evening Post* published 323 Rockwell covers, the last a portrait of President Kennedy. He titled his December 4, 1920 cover *Santa and Expense Book*. Along with his friend and neighbor Joseph Leyendecker, who painted 322 *Post* covers between 1899 and 1943, Rockwell helped popularize a realistic Santa—a bearded old man in a red suit, rather than the sometimes grotesque elf of Nast's cartoons. (Though Rockwell's Santa was not an elf, he *did* work with them. For the 1922 Christmas cover, he painted Claus dozing in a chair while eight doll-sized elves made toys and filled his sack.)

Rockwell painted more than 30 Santa covers, most of them for the *Saturday Evening Post*. One of the most popular, *Santa Consulting Globe*, appeared on December 4, 1926—his tenth cover that year. Holding a book titled *Good Boys*, Santa peers at the globe through a magnifying glass; cozy at home, he's wearing slippers and socks with his red suit and sleigh bells, and he has a writing quill tucked behind one ear. He also appears to have a halo, a reminder of his earlier life as Saint Nicholas.

Santa picked up a new prop—a distinctive glass bottle of soda pop—in 1931. Every year, Coca-Cola faced the same problem: people considered the bubbly drink a summer treat. When the temperature dropped, so did sales. For a solution, the company turned to advertising artist Haddon Sundblom.

Sundblom was born in Michigan in 1899, the youngest of ten children. When he was in eighth grade, his mother died and the family moved to Chicago, where he dropped out of school to help pay the bills. He began painting professionally in the early 1920s, at the Charles Everett Johnson Studio, one of Chicago's biggest advertising companies. To meet deadlines, he learned to finish oil paintings in a single sitting, adding fresh colors while the first layers were still wet.

By the time he started painting for Coca-Cola, Sundblom had his own busy studio in the Wrigley Building. Many of his students and assistants, including Gil Elvgren and Harold McCauley, became popular advertising and pinup artists.

(McCauley also posed for Sundblom's iconic portrait of the "Quaker Oats Man.")

It is only coincidence that Santa Claus wears the colors of the Coca-Cola logo. American children were well acquainted with the bearded old man in the red and white suit long before "Sunny" handed him a soft drink... but the season might not be as much fun without these paintings.

Haddon Sundblom painted Santa Claus for more than 30 years, from 1931 until 1964. His is the smiling, fun-loving Santa that little kids wait up for on Christmas Eve. Instead of obsessing over "naughty" and "nice" lists, this Santa makes time to play with the toy trains under your tree, to warm his feet by your fireplace, and to kick back in a favorite chair with a reindeer curled underneath like a faithful dog. Coca-Cola still uses his pictures for advertising, and in 2018, the United States Post Office put four of them on stamps (with the trademarked bottles cropped out).

For two decades years, Sundblom modeled his Santa Claus on his neighbor Lou Prentice, a former Coca-Cola salesman. After Prentice died, "Sunny" just drew the smiling face he saw in his mirror.

Reindeer Games

Aaron Montgomery Ward moved to Chicago in 1865, when he was 22. Traveling the Midwest as a salesman, he discovered that many rural customers believed they were overpaying for inferior products. His solution? Offer high-quality goods by mail and then ship them to local railroad stations, where customers could pick them up. In 1871, he filled a warehouse with merchandise, all paid for with cash.

Before he could sell any of it, the "Great Chicago Fire" carved a path through the city, a mile wide and four miles long. Most of the business district burned, including Ward's warehouse. Altogether, the fire claimed 17,000 buildings and 300 lives. Property damages hit $200 million.

Ward borrowed from friends to rebuild, and in 1872, distributed his first "catalog:" a single page listing 163 items and their prices. Though his two business partners abandoned him during the Panic of 1873 (a worldwide depression caused in part by the Great Fire), the business took off. Ward published a 32-page catalog in 1874 and began promising "satisfaction guaranteed or your money back" the following year. Montgomery Ward & Company recorded more than a million dollars in sales for 1879, and the catalog grew almost every year: 240 pages and 10,000 items in 1883, more than 600 pages and 25,000 items in 1895. Rural customers called it "The Wish Book."

The 1904 catalog weighed four pounds, but Montgomery Ward shipped more than three million of them. Since 1892, the company had been battling another Chicago-based catalog house: Sears, Roebuck & Company. In 1925, Sears converted part of its Chicago headquarters building to retail space.

Inset: 1876 Montgomery & Ward Company catalog

Aaron Ward had died in 1913. His successors opened the first Montgomery Ward store in 1926, in the small city of Plymouth, Indiana. By the time the stock market crashed in 1929, Ward had opened 531 stores, including a flagship on Chicago's Michigan Avenue. Sears, which had expanded just as rapidly, proposed a merger in 1930; Ward's executives declined.

In the late 1930s, Montgomery Ward was the nation's largest retailer. Every Christmas, the stores gave away millions of coloring books. For the 1939 season, management decided to publish their own children's book. To save money, they asked Robert May—a copywriter in the advertising department— to write it. May had never written for children before, but was known around the department for quickly composing witty limericks.

The company did not give him a lot of direction. The executives wanted a "cheery Christmas story." Inspired by the success of Munro Leaf's recent bestseller, *The Story of Ferdinand*, they suggested making an animal the main character. May selected a reindeer, mostly because his four-year-old daughter, Barbara, loved watching the deer at Chicago's Lincoln Park Zoo. He called his unlikely hero Rollo, and then Reginald, before settling on Rudolph.

May modeled his story partly on *The Ugly Duckling*, partly on his own childhood. As for the glowing red nose? One day as he watched a thick fog roll in off Lake Michigan, May imagined his hero using the light to guide Santa's sleigh through foul weather.

Reindeer live around the top of the world, from Scandinavia to Siberia and all across Alaska and Canada, where they are called Caribou. Though they don't range as far as the North Pole, and nobody has ever seen one fly, they have been associated with Santa Claus ever since Arthur Stansbury wrote *The Children's Friend* in 1821. Clement Moore was the first to give Santa a full team of "eight tiny reindeer," and to name them all.

In May's story, Rudolph did not grow up at the North Pole with Santa's team. Instead, he was born in a village inhabited entirely by reindeer—the kind that live in houses and spend their childhoods ice skating and playing hopscotch and leapfrog. Well, all except Rudolph; the other kids excluded him because his big red nose glowed in the dark.

Montgomery Ward executives almost made the same mistake. Their reasoning? No parent would give a child a book about a "red-nosed reindeer," because red noses were associated with excessive drinking!

May asked Denver Gillen, an in-house advertising artist, to go with him and Barbara to the Lincoln Park Zoo. Gillen's playful sketches of deer convinced the company bosses to publish May's fanciful story; they also gave Gillen the job of illustrating it.

Reindeer (vintage postcard)

During the 1939 Christmas season, Montgomery Ward stores gave away 2.4 million copies of *Rudolph the Red-Nosed Reindeer*. The first edition was a 32-page paperback, a little over ten inches tall. Gillen's pencil drawings, printed in red, blue, and brown, surrounded the rhymed text, which May had written in the same meter as Moore's *Visit*. Ward's executives and major suppliers received a limited-edition hardcover.

In the story, Santa lands on Rudolph's roof on a foggy Christmas Eve, behind schedule and badly shaken by a near-collision with an airplane. Spotting a red light in the window, he wakes the young reindeer and asks him to guide his sleigh the rest of the night. Rudolph writes a note for his parents, explaining his absence and telling them not to worry. When he returns in the morning, the story has spread and he is welcomed back as a hero.

Because of wartime paper shortages, Montgomery Ward did not reprint *Rudolph* until 1946, when they gave away another 3.6 million copies. The stores also carried all sorts of Rudolph merchandise that year, including toys, slippers, puzzles, and clothing.

In 1944, RCA Victor launched a "Youth Series" of 78 rpm records, featuring popular children's stories read over musical accompaniment. In the 1950s, these were rebranded as the "Little Nipper" series. Many of them were narrated by Paul Wing, an NBC radio writer and personality, whose *Spelling Bee* aired nationally in the late 1930s.

RCA executives wanted to record *Rudolph* in 1946, but the rights still belonged to Montgomery Ward. That changed the following year, when Ward's president, Sewell Avery, gave the copyright to Robert May. RCA released the poem on two ten-inch 78s. Paul Wing narrated over a musical score by George Kleinsinger, best known for composing *Tubby the Tuba*. NBC studio arranger Russ Case conducted the orchestra.

Robert May also shopped the book to major publishers. Most turned it down, convinced that Ward's had saturated the market by giving away six million paperbacks. But Maxton Publishers, a small New York company specializing in "Books for Little People," took a chance—and quickly sold out a hardcover first printing of 100,000 copies; a pop-up version followed in 1950. Vermont artist Marion Guild illustrated both editions.

Rudolph flew onto the nation's movie screens on November 11, 1948. Instead of a major Hollywood studio, the eight-minute cartoon was produced by the Jam Handy Organization, an industrial and educational filmmaker based in Detroit. Olympic swimmer Henry Jamison ("Jam") Handy had started the company in the early 1900s and produced military training films during the First World War. Afterwards, he did a lot of work for General Motors.

Handy brought in legendary animator Max Fleischer to bring May's reindeer to life. Max Fleischer and his brother Dave began making their innovative *Out of the Inkwell* cartoons, featuring Koko the Clown, shortly after the War. By the 1930s, the Fleischers were turning out a short every week, including the popular *Betty Boop* and *Popeye* cartoons. They also released two full-length animated features and, in the early 1940s, a series of full-color, ten-minute *Superman* adventures. The animators thought Superman looked silly "leaping" over tall buildings, and got permission from his creators to make him fly instead.

Paul Wing returned to narrate this Technicolor *Rudolph*. The film closely followed May's book, and even incorporated a lot of his original text. (The cartoon is free to watch online.)

Santa and Reindeer (vintage Christmas card

But the best was still to come. Robert May's sister, Margaret, married New York songwriter Johnny Marks in 1947. Marks had first considered *Rudolph the Red-Nosed Reindeer* as a possible song title in 1939. Ten years later, he finally set a simplified version of May's story to music.

Convinced he had written a hit, Marks pitched *Rudolph* to the year's biggest stars, including Bing Crosby, Perry Como, and Dinah Shore. They all turned the song down.

So did Gene Autry, one of the silver screen's most popular singing cowboys. In 1946, Autry had ridden his horse Champion through the streets of Los Angeles, at the head of the annual Santa Claus Lane Parade. All along the route, people chanted, "Here Comes Santa Claus." Autry expanded the chant into a lyric, which composer Oakley Haldeman set to music. The following December, Autry's record of *Here Comes Santa Claus (Down Santa Claus Lane)* hit #9 on the pop chart and cracked the country top five. By 1949, he was looking for another Christmas hit—but he was sure *Rudolph* wouldn't be it. His wife, Ina, disagreed.

Autry cut *Rudolph the Red-Nosed Reindeer* in one take at the end of a recording session. Ina convinced him to put it on the B-Side of his 1949 single, *If it Doesn't Snow on Christmas*. But Marks (and Ina May Autry) had guessed right; *Rudolph* was the hit, selling almost two million copies that Christmas season. When Columbia rereleased the single in 1950, the reindeer got the A-side.

All these successes turned Robert May's life around. He was still writing ads for Montgomery Ward in the late 1940s, trying to pay off medical debts; his wife had died in the summer of 1939 after a two-year battle with cancer.

May finally left Ward's in 1950 to build The Rudolph Company, which still manages the reindeer's licensing empire. Though he sometimes joked that he spent his life "working for a reindeer," May displayed a life-sized Rudolph statue on his front lawn every Christmas. Since 1982, the statue has hung above the rare books library at Dartmouth College, from which May graduated in 1926.

Meanwhile, May's brother-in-law was making a name for himself as a writer of popular Christmas songs. In 1956, Johnny Marks set the 1863 Longfellow poem *Christmas Bells* to music and retitled it *I Heard the Bells on Christmas Day*. Bing Crosby cut the song that October and released it as a holiday single; Frank Sinatra also recorded it, as did Kate Smith, Sarah McLachlan, The Carpenters, and many others. Marks also wrote *Rockin' Around the Christmas Tree*, which Brenda Lee recorded in 1958, when she was just thirteen; the song hit the charts two years later.

A recording of *Rudolph the Red-Nosed Reindeer* was inserted under the opening and closing titles of the Fleischer cartoon when it was rereleased in 1951. But Marks was skeptical when he first heard plans to use his song as the basis for an hour-long television special.

General Electric was looking for a way to promote housewares at Christmastime. Advertising executive William Sahloff, who had worked with Robert May at Montgomery Ward, suggested adapting *Rudolph*. For television producers Arthur Rankin, Jr. and Jules Bass, the magical tale sounded like the perfect showcase for the stop-motion "Animagic" process they were developing with Japanese animator Tadahito Mochinaga.

In the early 60s, both Rankin and Marks lived in New York's Greenwich Village. Rankin convinced Marks to let them use his hit song, and to write several others. Screenwriter Romeo Muller, who had started writing and performing marionette plays when he was eleven years old, based the script on Marks's lyric, rather than May's book. To flesh out the story, Muller added most of the special's iconic characters, including Hermey the Elf, prospector Yukon Cornelius, the Misfit Toys, and of course, the Abominable Snowmonster (or "Bumble," as Cornelius calls it). Music and dialogue were recorded in Toronto, but all the animation was done in Japan.

The film took a year and a half to make and cost half a million dollars. Puppet makers Kyoko Kita and Ichoro Komuro created dozens of tiny figures, most of them less than a foot tall. Santa stood nine inches, his elves no more than six or eight; the adult reindeer were twelve inches long. They were made mostly of wood and rubber, attached to flexible wire armatures. Rudolph's nose was a 12-volt bulb.

Stop-motion animation is photographed one frame at a time. Between frames, each puppet is moved or adjusted, ever so slightly, to create the illusion of continuous motion. For each shot, one animator was assigned to each character. Most of the crew was new to animation, and learning on the job. Along with the special, they also animated three 60-second commercials for General Electric, in which Santa's elves wrapped electric can openers, toothbrushes, and toaster ovens.

Rudolph the Red-Nosed Reindeer premiered on Sunday, December 6, 1964. Though the special played against an NFL game in some markets, more than half of the national audience tuned in. The show was so popular that for 1965, rival network ABC commissioned *A Charlie Brown Christmas*. *How the Grinch Stole Christmas*, based on the Dr. Seuss book and directed by *Looney Tunes* animator Chuck Jones, first aired in 1966.

Actor and folksinger Burl Ives, who narrated *Rudolph* as Sam the Snowman, rerecorded three songs from the special for his 1965 album, *Have a Holly Jolly Christmas*. Rankin/Bass went on to produce a long string of animated holiday specials, including *Santa Claus is Comin' to Town*, *Frosty the Snowman*, *Here Comes Peter Cottontail*, and several Rudolph and Frosty sequels. Romeo Muller wrote all of them, as well as the 1977 Rankin/Bass adaptation of Tolkien's *The Hobbit*.

O Christmas Tree

Woodsman Mike Carr cut down 36 evergreens in December, 1851. With his two sons, he bundled the trees into wagons and hauled them down from the Catskill Mountains to Hoboken, where he caught a ferry to New York. He arrived on the 20th, the Saturday before Christmas.

The papers said New Yorkers were venturing into the countryside to cut trees to decorate for the holidays. Carr took a chance and paid a dollar to rent a spot on the sidewalk in Washington Market, at the corner of Greenwich and Vesey Streets. There, surrounded by farm stalls and food vendors, he set up the city's first Christmas tree sales lot; ten cents for his smallest trees, a quarter for the eight- and ten-footers.

Christmas trees were still a new idea in the United States. You won't find one in Irving's *History* or Moore's *Visit*. German families imported the custom in the 1820s, but it would not spread beyond their rural communities until the second half of the nineteenth century.

One of the first American depictions of a Christmas tree appeared in the December 1850 issue of *Godey's Lady's Book*. Louis Godey had started publishing the fashion monthly in 1830. For the first few years, he filled it mostly with reprints of French magazine articles and illustrations.

The *Lady's Book* had only 10,000 monthly subscribers in 1837, when Godey hired Sarah Josepha Hale as editor. A novelist, essayist, and poet, Hale ran the magazine for the next 40 years. She published only original works by American writers, including Edgar Allen Poe, Harriet Beecher Stowe, and Ralph Waldo Emerson; three issues were written entirely by American women. Circulation climbed to 70,000 in the 1840s and peaked at 150,000 in 1860.

Every issue included a hand-colored fashion plate, along with patterns for women's clothing and needlework projects. The 1850 Christmas issue also featured an engraving of a young family gathered around a richly-decorated table-top spruce. The picture was widely distributed in the 1850s, and *Godey's* reprinted it in December, 1860.

Hale filled *Godey's* with American writers and themes, and asked five different presidents to make

Thanksgiving a National Holiday (Abraham Lincoln finally took her advice in 1863, declaring the fourth Thursday in November a "National Day of Thanksgiving"). But for the model of feminine virtue, Hale directed her readers' attention across the Atlantic.

Queen Victoria was crowned on June 20, 1837, a month after she turned 18. She married her first cousin, Prince Albert of Saxe-Coburg and Gotha (now part of Bavaria) in February, 1840. They had nine children before Albert died of typhoid fever in December, 1861, at the age of 42. Their first son, Albert Edward, would become King Edward VII when Victoria died in 1901.

Victoria grew up with German Christmas traditions, included decorated trees. Her grandmother, Queen Charlotte, was born in Mecklenburg-Strelitz, in northern Germany. When she married George III in 1761, she was seventeen and did not speak a word of English. Though Charlotte soon learned her husband's language, she also introduced him to her family's tradition of decorating an evergreen branch every Christmas. In 1800, she decorated an entire English Yew tree instead, and surrounded it with gifts for all the royal children at Windsor. The custom spread quickly, at least among the upper classes.

Victoria and Albert's Christmas tree
Godey's Lady's Book, 1850

George and Charlotte's first two sons were crowned George IV and William IV. Their fourth, Edward, married Victoria Maria Louisa of Sax-Coburg, whose brother would become King Leopold I of Belgium in 1831. Queen Victoria was Edward and Victoria's only child.

The first written description of a Christmas tree dates back to 1510. On Christmas Eve, merchants in the Latvian town of Riga decorated a small evergreen with artificial roses to honor the Virgin Mary. By the 1530s, when Alsace was part of Germany, merchants were selling cut trees in town markets. Buyers set them up on tables, undecorated. Princess Helene de Mecklembourg decorated the first Christmas tree in Paris in 1837, after she married Ferdinand, the eldest son of the Duke of Orleans.

Because they are the only plants that keep their colors during the northern winters, evergreens have been associated with winter festivals since ancient times. Celts, Greeks, and Romans assigned magical or healing properties to holly, yew, and mistletoe (which is both parasitic and poisonous).

Celts wore holly in their hair to chase away evil spirits. Roman soldiers brought it back from the British Isles to decorate their homes during Saturnalia, their week-long, gift-giving winter holiday. To avoid suspicion, early Christians under Roman rule continued hanging holly during

Saturnalia. But they associated the red of the berries with Christ's blood, and the points on the leaves with the thorns in his crown (one Scandinavian name for holly translates as "Christ's thorns").

Holly and Mistletoe – Vintage Christmas card

The Scandinavians may also have been the first to bring evergreens into their homes during the winter festival. Vikings hung the trees upside down from their roof beams.

Growing up in Saxe-Coburg, Prince Albert loved singing carols and decorating small, table-top trees. After he married Victoria, she encouraged him to share these traditions with their children. So he imported trees from Coburg and decorated them himself with candles, sweets, toys, dolls, and German glass ornaments.

In 1848, the *London Illustrated News* published a 16-page Christmas supplement. The most popular woodcut showed Victoria, Albert, and their five young children standing around a decorated tree. Overnight, trees became part of the British Christmas.

Sarah Hale commissioned a copy of this drawing for the December 1850 *Godey's Lady's Book*. To "Americanize" the image, the artist removed Victoria's tiara and Albert's mustache; otherwise, the pictures are almost identical.

So the following season, Mark Carr sold all 36 of his trees. He returned to Washington Market with a fresh haul each December for the rest of his life, and his sons were still selling trees there in the late 1890s. By then, they had plenty of competition. In 1880, a *New York Times* reporter estimated there were 200,000 trees for sale in the city. As late as the 1930s, most of the lots were still on the Lower West Side, near the docks.

Franklin Pierce was the first president to decorate a Christmas tree. He set it up outside the White House in 1856, for the city's Sunday School students. The government did not officially recognize Christmas as a holiday until fourteen years later, in 1870!

New York Christmas tree lot, 1903

Theodore Roosevelt tried to reverse the trend in 1901. Concerned that annual evergreen harvests were depleting the nation's forests, he banned Christmas trees from his White House. Disappointed, his sons snuck one in and decorated it in a closet. Though their ingenuity amused him, TR brought them to Gifford Pinchot, chief of the Division of Forestry, for a lecture on conservation. Pinchot surprised his boss by siding with the boys. But despite Pinchot's assurances that a certain amount of cutting was actually beneficial for well-managed forests, Roosevelt never displayed a tree during his presidency.

Similar concerns inspired German manufacturers to produce artificial trees in the 1880s. The branches were made of goose feathers, dyed green and stiffened with wire. Sears began selling "feather trees" in 1883, ranging in price from 50 cents to a dollar; the 1913 catalog listed artificial trees ranging in height from 17 inches to 55. British manufacturers introduced trees made of dyed brush bristles in the 1920s, and a Chicago company began selling aluminum trees in 1956. Today, most artificial trees are made in China of colored PVC plastic.

William McGalliard studied business before going to work on his family's farm in Hamilton Township, New Jersey, a few miles from Trenton. In 1901, he found a use for ten nearly worthless acres. Instead of the usual crops, which wouldn't grow in the rocky soil, he planted 25,000 Norway spruce. He began harvesting the trees seven years later, and sold them for a dollar apiece. There are now more than 15,000 Christmas tree farms in the United States. Between them, they grow about 90% of the trees sold each December.

Franklin Roosevelt started growing Christmas trees at his Hyde Park estate in 1926. By the 1940s, his secretary was advertising them to department store buyers. FDR also gave trees to his friends. "One to be shipped to the Crown Princess of Norway at Bethesda, Maryland," he wrote in October, 1943, "and one for Prime Minister Winston Churchill, on which I will give you shipping directions later."

Facing Page:
Santa with toys and Christmas tree
Harper's New Monthly Magazine, 1896

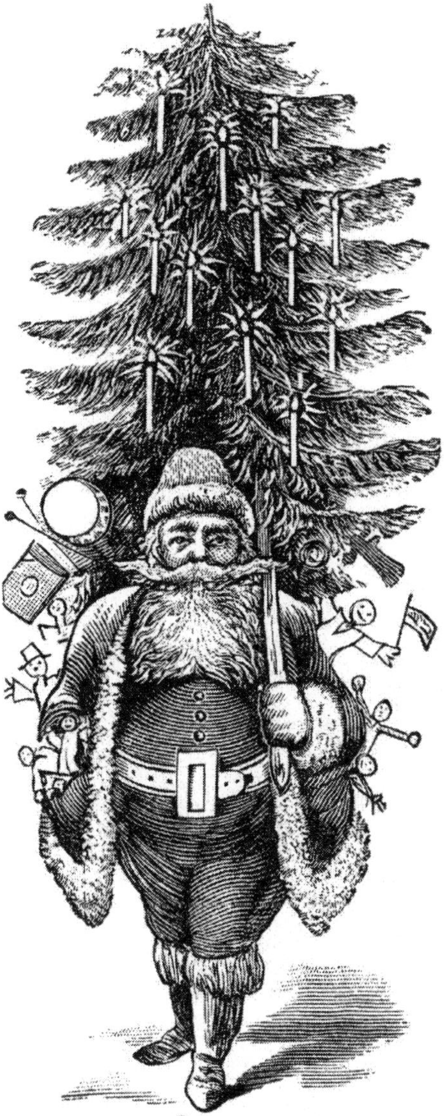

Vintage Poinsettia Christmas card

Two popular Christmas plants are native to the Americas.

Joel Poinsett, the first United States Minister to Mexico, discovered *Euphorbia Pulcherrima* at a Catholic Christmas mass in 1824. Mexican friars called the red and green shrub *Flor de Noche Buena*, "Christmas Eve Flower." Poinsett brought some seeds home to South Carolina, where they were grown in greenhouses to be displayed in Charleston churches. Historian William Prescott, who wrote about Poinsett in *The History of the Conquest of Mexico* (1843), named the plant "Poinsettia" in his honor.

European botanists began growing *Schlumbergera*, a cactus native to the mountains of coastal Brazil, in 1818. (French botanist and author

Charles Lemaire named the species after Frederic Schlumberger, who collected rare cacti.) English flower sellers came up with a more marketable name in the 1950s; because the red flowers blossom in late November, they called *Schlumbergera* the "Christmas Cactus." (Here in the United States, it is also sold as "Thanksgiving Cactus.")

Schlumbergera – 1839 botanical print

Let There Be Lights

Most pictures of Victorian Christmas trees show the branches decorated with lighted candles. Some believe this tradition began in Germany with Martin Luther. The story goes that Luther was walking home on a winter's night. He found himself captivated by the starlight twinkling through the evergreens, and wanted to share the magic with his family and friends. So he cut down a small tree, set it up on a table at home, and attached candle holders to the tips of the branches.

Though there are woodcut illustrations of Luther and his family gathered around a candlelit tree, the story is probably apocryphal. Luther never mentions it in his own writings, and the pictures were made centuries after he died.

Martin Luther's Christmas tree (antique woodcut)

Regardless of who started the tradition, it survived into the first decades of the twentieth century. This is why Victorian trees were trimmed into widely-spaced tiers: so the flames would not ignite the branches above. (The removed branches were used to make wreaths and other decorations.) Early artificial trees were designed the same way, often with candle-holders built into the ends of the branches. Sometimes the holders were disguised as berries.

Of course candles and trees—real or artificial—were a dangerous combination. By early 1900s, you could buy counterbalanced holders that were almost impossible to tip and glass globes or lanterns to contain the flames. But the candles could still only be lit for short periods of time, and only a fool would leave them unattended.

As the popularity of Christmas trees increased, so did the number of seasonal fires. In 1908, American insurance companies began lobbying for laws banning candlelit trees.

That December, Ralph Morris saw his son accidently tip one of the candles on their tree. Though he moved quickly enough to prevent disaster, Morris decided it was time for a safer decoration. By attaching the miniature lights and wiring from an old telephone switchboard to a feather tree, he created what was probably the world's first "pre-lit" Christmas tree.

Edward Hibberd Johnson moved to New York in 1871 to manage the Automatic Telegraph Company. The electric telegraph was the fastest communication system yet devised. But messages could only be sent as quickly as human operators could tap them out in Morse code. For a skilled operator, that was about 25 to 40 words per minute; fast enough for short notes, but impractical for lengthy reports or newspaper dispatches.

One of Johnson's first hires was a 24-year-old inventor, Thomas Alva Edison. Eating and sleeping at his desk, Edison reviewed everything the company's engineers had already tried, and then launched his own exhaustive series of experiments.

Thomas Edison's Menlo Park "Invention Factory," painted in the winter of 1880-81 by R.F. Outcault

Edison solved the company's problem in just six weeks. By 1874, he had designed machines able to transmit and receive up to 1,000 words a minute.

Johnson helped Edison open an "Invention Factory" in Menlo Park, New Jersey in March 1876, and then spent the next two years promoting the phonograph and an improved telephone. Edison applied for his first electric light patent on October 5, 1878 and incorporated the Edison Electric Light Company less than two weeks later. The public got its first look at the bulb in December, 1879. The following December, Edison decorated the outside of his lab with a string of electric lights.

Edison closed the Menlo Park facility in 1881 and moved to New York. With Johnson, he organized the Edison Electric Illuminating

Company to build a generating station on Pearl Street in lower Manhattan. When the station was switched on in September 1882, it had only 82 customers. Two years later, 508 customers were connected, all in the same few blocks; the direct current lines could only carry power short distances.

So Edward Johnson, who lived on East 36th Street, had to install a generator in his basement. He experimented with concealed wiring and ambient lighting, and on December 22, 1882, he invited reporters to see his Christmas tree. Only one showed up: William Augustus Croffut, who wrote for the *Detroit Post and Tribune*.

"It was brilliantly lighted," Croffut wrote.

with many colored globes about as large as an English walnut and was turning some six times a minute on a little pine box. There were eighty lights in all encased in these dainty glass eggs, and about equally divided between white, red and blue. As the tree turned, the colors alternated ... a continuous twinkling of dancing colors, red, white and blue, all evening ... one can hardly imagine anything prettier.

Johnson had also hung two strings of lights from his ceiling. The whole display was visible from the street through his parlor windows, so passerby stopped to stare.

The *New York Times* finally sent a reporter during the 1884 Christmas season. Under the headline *A Brilliant Christmas Tree – How an Electrician Amused His Children*, New Yorkers read about a six-foot revolving tree decorated with 120 colored bulbs. Johnson also had electric chandeliers, and the fire in his parlor was an illusion created by "colored paper ... under which electric lights are hidden." Most impressively, the basement dynamo "makes so little noise that it can not be heard on the floor above."

The Edison General Electric Company wired the White House for power in 1891. The generator was next door, in the basement of the State, War, and Navy Building. Uncomfortable with the strange new technology, President Benjamin Harrison refused to touch the switches; he and his wife relied on the household staff to turn the lights on and off.

Grover Cleveland, whom Harrison had defeated in the 1888 election, returned to the White House in 1893. Each Christmas, he displayed a decorated tree in the Blue Room. The tradition was only a few years old; Harrison first displayed a tree there in 1889. For the 1895 season, Cleveland had the tree decorated with gold angels, silver sleds, and—a White House first—hundreds of colored lights.

Suddenly, electric Christmas lights were fashionable.

Grover Cleveland's White House Christmas tree, 1895

Of course, only the wealthy could afford them. Bulbs cost a dollar apiece, and you had to hire an electrician to wire them together. There were no sockets yet; no wall outlets, either. And power stations were still so rare, you might have to install your own generator. So lighting a single tree could cost up to $300—several thousand in 2018 money.

The Edison General Electric Company began advertising Christmas tree lights in December, 1901. Each "festoon" of eight miniature bulbs cost $12, or you could rent it for the season for $1.50. Because they were so expensive, the lights were mostly used to decorate department store windows.

Early print campaigns were anything but subtle, trumpeting "No Danger." One featured two drawings: a tree safely lit with Edison lamps, and a candlelit tree bursting into flame. More sophisticated ads followed, and GE offered strings of 8, 16, 24, or even 32 bulbs. Prices remained high until the 1920s, when competition increased.

Russian immigrant Conrad Hubert started the American Electrical Novelty and Manufacturing Company in 1896. His first catalogs were heavy on the novelties, including battery-powered necktie and scarf pins; for Halloween, you could get a lighted pin shaped like a skull or a Jack-o'-lantern. In 1899, he began selling a more practical device: a carbon filament lamp and a brass reflector, set into the end of a cardboard tube that held two D-batteries. Because the lamp drew so much power that it could only be used in short bursts, Hubert marketed it as a "Flash Light." Despite its limitations, the gadget sold well to police departments.

Hubert displayed a variety of products at the 1904 St. Louis World's Fair, including reading lamps, bicycle lights, and electric candles. He renamed the business "The American Ever Ready Company" in 1905, introduced a more efficient tungsten filament flashlight bulb in 1907, and began selling boxes of Christmas tree lights in 1912. Though the lights were less expensive than GE's, they never had a chance to make much of an impact. American Ever Ready became part of battery manufacturer The National Carbon Company in 1914. Three years later, Union Carbide bought National Carbon and discontinued the lighting and novelty divisions to focus on its battery brands: Eveready and Energizer.

The Sadacca family came to New York from Spain in the early 1900s. By 1914, they had a small novelty shop. One of their most popular items was a birdcage lantern; inside the wicker cage was a fake bird containing a small electric light.

In 1917, Albert Sadacca read about a tragic fire caused by Christmas tree candles. The 15-year-old suggested to his parents that they string together some of their extra lightbulbs and sell them as a safe alternative to candles. That first season, the family sold 100 strings of white lights. The business exploded the following year, when Albert began painting the bulbs festive colors.

By the early 1920s, more than a dozen manufacturers were selling electric Christmas lights, including The Interstate Electric Novelty Company, the Five Seas Trading Company (which imported fancy bulbs from Austria), and C.D. Wood Electric. (The Patent Office had rejected GE's application for "festoons," on the grounds that every electrician knew how to string bulbs together.)

Lester Haft, an engineer working for C.D. Wood Electric, applied for a patent in March, 1921. His invention? A tri-plug connector that made it possible to connect strings of Christmas lights end to end, so that multiple strings could be plugged into a single outlet. After the patent was approved in October, 1924, every manufacturer that wanted to sell connectible strings had to pay a licensing fee.

General Electric and Westinghouse had recently begun offering affordable Christmas lights; the GE sets had long-lasting, tungsten-filament MAZDA bulbs shaped like flames. To compete with these giants, Albert Sadacca and his brothers, Leon and Henri, invited more than a dozen rivals to join a new trade organization: the National Outfit Manufacturer's Association. NOMA, for short. Most agreed, and in 1926, they all merged to form the NOMA Electric Company.

The time was right. On Christmas Eve, 1923, President Calvin Coolidge lit the first National Christmas Tree on the White House lawn. The ceremony began at three in the afternoon, with a two hour concert by the First Congregational

Church Choir, 100 voices strong. At five, Coolidge walked out and pressed a button under the tree to turn on the 3,000 electric lights. No speech; not from "Silent Cal." Afterwards, thousands of DC residents gathered on the lawn to enjoy the tree and sing carols well into the night.

In January 1925, Coolidge would tell the Society of American Newspaper Editors, "The chief business of the American people is business." The organizers of the 1923 lighting would not have disagreed. Before going to work for Commerce Secretary Herbert Hoover, Frederick Morris Feiker edited the trade journals *Electrical World* and *Electrical Merchandising*. He suggested the lighting as a way to promote the electrical industry—including the companies that made electric Christmas lights. After Hoover brought Coolidge on board, the Electric League of Washington agreed to donate the colored bulbs; other manufacturers provided $5,000 worth of wiring.

The plan worked. Sales of electric Christmas lights soared in the late 1920s. NOMA dominated the industry until the 1960s, when the company filed for bankruptcy. Sales had dropped in the 1950s, when aluminum trees became fashionable; because the metal limbs conducted electricity, they could not be decorated with strings of lights. Instead, people illuminated the trees from underneath with revolving "color wheels." By the time aluminum trees fell out of favor in the 1960s, importers had flooded the market with the cheap "mini lights" we still use today... or will, until they're all replaced with more efficient LEDs.

Renamed the "National Community Christmas Tree" in 1924, the tree on the White House lawn remains one of the nation's most popular traditions. Accompanied by British Prime Minister Winston Churchill, Franklin Roosevelt addressed a national radio audience before the 1941 lighting:

When we make ready our hearts for the labor and the suffering and the ultimate victory which lie ahead, then we observe Christmas Day – with all of its memories and all of its meanings – as we should.

The tree was next lit on December 24, 1945, to celebrate that "ultimate victory."

Christmas at the Rock

New York was in the middle of a building boom when the stock market crashed in October, 1929. Developers finished the buildings that were already under construction, including the Chrysler and the Empire State. But by December 1931, 64% of the city's construction workers were unemployed.

Most of those who still had jobs were working on the same project. Fortunately, it was a big one that would take the rest of the decade: twelve acres spread over three city blocks, 48th to 51st between Fifth and Sixth Avenues. In 1929, there were more than 200 old buildings on these blocks, many with basement speakeasies. As their leases expired, the buildings were vacated. By 1930, demolition crews were tearing them down and carting away the debris.

John D. Rockefeller, Jr. had leased the property from Columbia University to build Metropolitan Square, a "city within a city" anchored by a grand new home for the Metropolitan Opera. But when the Met backed out after the Crash, Junior had to send the architects back to their drawing boards. The place also needed a new name. After much debate, his advisors convinced him the family name would attract major tenants, and Rockefeller Center was born.

On Christmas Eve, 1931, the property was a muddy wasteland. But a group of grateful workers set up a 20-foot balsam fir and decorated it with homemade garlands and tin cans. At the end of the day, they lined up at the tree to collect their pay.

Public relations director Merle Crowell launched an annual tradition in November, 1933. The first official Rockefeller Center Christmas tree was a 50-foot evergreen decorated with 700 electric lights, standing on a platform in front of the just-completed RCA Building (30 Rockefeller Plaza). The lighting ceremony, which featured choirs and a female trumpet trio, was recorded for broadcast on the NBC radio network.

In true New York City fashion, the 1934 tree was even taller and brighter: a 70-foot Norway spruce, illuminated by four floodlights and strung with 1,200 electric bulbs. Radio City Music Hall organist Richard Leibert performed at the December 11 lighting ceremony.

Rockefeller Center Christmas tree and *Prometheus* statue, photographed in December, 2001

Radio City Music Hall and the RKO Building

"In its architecture Rockefeller Center stands as distinctively for New York as the Louvre stands for Paris."

"Nearly everything about the Music Hall is tremendous. It seats 6,200 patrons ... staff of 600 employees ... the world's largest theater orchestra, and the screen, seventy feet by forty, is the world's largest."

Federal Writers' Project
New York City Guide (1939)

Rockefeller Center, Channel Gardens view
Left to right: *La Maison Francaise*, the Comcast Building (30 Rockefeller Plaza) and the British Empire Building

Saint Patrick's Cathedral, from Rockefeller Center

The RCA Building—actually, the Comcast Building since 2015—is still the tallest in Rockefeller Center: 66 stories, 872 feet. The public observation deck opened in July 1933, the Rainbow Room a year later; express elevators will get you to either one in less than a minute.

Filled with corporate offices and NBC radio and television studios, 30 Rockefeller overlooks a sunken plaza decorated with Paul Manship's bronze statue of the Greek god *Prometheus*. Lined with shops and restaurants, the plaza was supposed to be the outdoor heart of Rockefeller Center. But after just a few years, the shops were failing.

John D. Rockefeller, Jr. found another use for the plaza in 1936. That December, engineer M.R. Carpenter installed a system of pipes that transformed the concrete floor into a temporary ice skating rink.

When the rink opened on Christmas Day, Omero Catan was first in line for a ticket. Nicknamed "Mr. First," Catan would have it no other way. As a child, he had met a man who walked across the Brooklyn Bridge the day it opened in 1883. Catan attended more than 500 openings in his life, paying the first tolls on both levels of the George Washington Bridge; buying the first token for the Eighth Avenue Subway; and putting the first coin in a New York City parking meter. He and his brother rode the first plane to land at Idlewild (now LaGuardia) Airport, and in December 1937, he waited a day and a half in Weehawken, New Jersey to take the first drive through the Lincoln Tunnel.

In 1936, and again in '37, Rockefeller Center had two Christmas trees: twin 70-foot Norway spruce, standing side-by-side above the plaza. Visitors in 1942 saw an even more unusual display: three Norway spruce from Huntington, Long Island. The one in the middle was 50 feet tall, the others 30. All three were topped with stars and decorated with colored balls, red on one tree, blue and white on the others. Due to wartime blackouts and power rationing, no lights were hung.

Since 1943, the Center has displayed one giant tree every Christmas. Executives begin looking for the "perfect" tree—at least 65 feet tall and 35 wide—early each year, and usually make their choice by July 4. The trees are driven into Manhattan overnight, to avoid backing up traffic. Most have been Norway spruce—a few were white spruce or balsam fir—and have come from nine different states, including New York, New Jersey, Connecticut, Maine, Massachusetts, Vermont, New Hampshire, and Pennsylvania. The 1998 tree was flown by cargo plane from Ohio, and the 1966 tree was brought down from Canada. The tallest to date was a 100-foot Norway spruce cut in Killingworth, Connecticut in 1999; the 10-ton tree was delivered to Manhattan on a barge, because it was too big to fit through the Lincoln Tunnel.

Once a tree arrives, decorating it can take up to a week. Much of the work—including attaching the star—is done before the tree is raised vertical. (The toppers have always been stars. Since 2004, they have been made of Swarovski crystal and lit by LEDs; the 2004 star was nine feet in diameter and weighed 550 pounds.) Every year since 2007, the trees have been lit entirely by LEDs. All of the power is supplied by solar panels on the roof of 45 Rockefeller Plaza, the 39-story skyscraper across from Saint Patrick's Cathedral (Lee Lawrie's bronze *Atlas* stands in the Fifth Avenue courtyard).

The tree is usually lit on the first Wednesday after Thanksgiving. Though the ceremony has been televised every year since 1951, the performances were not broadcast live until 1997. Headliners that year included the Rockettes, saxophonist Kenny G, and singer Harry Connick, Jr.

The tree is lowered again at the end of the season, so the star and lights can be removed. The Center began recycling trees in the early 1970s, in response to the growing environmental movement. Most are ground up and used as mulch in city parks or Boy Scout camps. One trunk became the mast of a sailing ship; others have been cut into planks for Habitat for Humanity, or donated to the United States Equestrian Team for horse jumps.

In 1954, sculptor Valerie Clarebout fashioned a dozen angels out of aluminum wire. Painted white and filled with electric lights, they were arranged in two rows in the middle of the Channel Gardens, the broad walkway sloping down from Fifth Avenue to the skating rink. (The space is called the "Channel" because it passes between the British Empire Building and *La Maison Francaise*, two six-story office and retail buildings completed in 1934.) Over the next decade, Clarebout created a variety of Christmas decorations for the gardens, including lighted snowmen, reindeer, and animated jack-in-the-boxes. She made a new set of angels, eight feet tall and sturdier than the originals, in 1969. With minor repairs and adjustments, they have been displayed every year since. Each holds a long brass horn, and no two are exactly alike.

Radio City Music Hall opened December 27, 1932. The variety show that night started at eight and ran until two in the morning. Few stayed to the end, and in the city's papers, the building got better reviews than the entertainment.

Management switched to a new format on January 11, 1933: a stage show followed by a feature film. Even this got off to a slow start. Frank Capra's Chinese Civil War drama, *The Bitter Tea of General Yen*, scheduled to play for two weeks, was replaced after just eight days. Barbara Stanwyck, who played a missionary rescued by a Chinese general, blamed racism for the poor box office.

Many of the movies that opened at Radio City were made or distributed by RKO Radio Pictures, which had its headquarters in the adjoining skyscraper. The studio's hits that first year included *King Kong*, which played the Hall in March. On November 16, more than 20,000 people braved the cold for the opening of George Cukor's adaptation of *Little Women*, starring Katherine Hepburn. In just three weeks, *Little Women* sold 450,701 tickets at the Music Hall, including a one-day record of 30,010 on Saturday, December 2.

RKO also released Walt Disney's cartoons, including the innovative *Silly Symphony* series. *The Three Little Pigs*, which won Best Animated Short at the 1934 Academy Awards, opened on May 27, 1933; *Who's Afraid of the Big, Bad Wolf* quickly became the studio's first hit song.

Disney's *The Night Before Christmas*, based loosely on Moore's poem, opened on December 21, 1933, along with the RKO feature *Flying Down to Rio*—the first movie in which Fred Astaire danced with Ginger Rogers. Both pictures were hits. *Rio* has a dance sequence staged on the wings of flying airplanes. In *The Night Before Christmas*, Santa delivers a Christmas tree and unleashes an army of animated toys—including a wind-up Mickey Mouse—to decorate it; toy soldiers shoot the colored balls onto the branches with cannons, and a miniature blimp lowers the topper into place.

Movies played four times a day at Radio City. Before the movie, audiences saw an elaborate stage show featuring the Hall's precision dance troupe, then known as The Roxyettes. Management built a new show each time the movies changed—about once every two weeks. To learn the new routines, the dancers began rehearsing every morning at seven.

The Adoration of the Shepherds (1622)
Dutch Nativity painting by Gerard van Honthorst
(Wallraf-Richartz Museum, in Cologne, Germany)

For December 21, 1933, producer Leon Leonidoff, choreographer Russell Markert, and stage designer Vincent Minnelli created the first *Christmas Spectacular*. The show included solo performances by tenor Jan Peerce and organist Richard Leibert, along with two segments that have anchored every Radio City Christmas show since: The Living Nativity and *The Parade of the Wooden Soldiers*.

The tradition of the Living Nativity began in 1223, when Saint Francis of Assisi delivered a Christmas sermon in a cave near the medieval Italian town of Greccio. Behind him, an infant slept in a hay-filled manger, watched over by people dressed as Mary, Joseph and a group of shepherds; a donkey and an ox completed the scene. The Music Hall Nativity adds the colorful procession of the Wise Men, bringing their gifts from the East. From the start, the Radio City show has incorporated live animals; in 2017, two sheep, three camels, and a donkey.

German operetta composer Leon Jessel wrote *Die Parade de Zinnsoldaten—"The Parade of the Tin Soldiers"*—as a piano solo in 1897; an orchestral version followed in 1905. Russian choreographer Nikita Balieff renamed it *The Parade of the Wooden Soldiers* for his 1911 vaudeville review *La Chauve-Souris ("The Bat")*, which played New York in 1922. Bandleaders including John Philip Sousa added the march to their shows, Paul Whiteman cut a hit record with his orchestra in 1923, and Broadway lyricist Ballard MacDonald added words in the 1920s; The Crystals sang them on *A Christmas Gift for You from Phil Spector* (1963).

In 1933, Fleischer Studios released a bizarre Betty Boop cartoon titled *Parade of the Wooden Soldiers*. After a brief clip of NBC radio violinist David Rubinoff playing the tune with his orchestra, a Betty doll arrives at a toy store, where she has to be rescued from a rampaging, Kong-like stuffed ape by an army of toy soldiers; Jessel's music underscores the mayhem.

That same year, Radio City choreographer Russell Markert adapted Balieff's dance routine for the Roxyettes. Inspired by the precision dancing in the 1922 *Ziegfeld Follies*, Markert assembled his first dance troupe in St. Louis in 1925. When he brought them to New York a few years later, he changed their name from The Missouri Rockets to The American Rockets. Samuel "Roxy" Rothafel renamed them the Roxyettes after he booked them into his enormous Roxy Theatre on Times Square.

Rothafel joined the Rockefeller Center advisory board in 1930 and helped to design Radio City Music Hall. When the Hall opened two years later, he brought the Roxyettes with him. By then, the line had grown from 16 dancers to 36. Since 1934, they have been known as the Radio City Music Hall Rockettes. They made their first television appearance in 1950, and began performing in the annual Macy's Thanksgiving Day Parade in 1957.

Before Radio City abandoned the stage show-and-a-movie format in the late 1970s, more than 700 pictures premiered there, including *White Christmas*, *Breakfast at Tiffany's*, *The Sound of Music*, and *Mary Poppins*. In the 1980s, *The Radio City Christmas Spectacular Starring the Rockettes* was reinvented as a 90-minute stage show, featuring up to 140 performers; though the show changes annually, every performance includes *Parade of the Wooden Soldiers* and ends with The Living Nativity.

34th Street Miracles

Miracle on 34th Street opened at New York's Roxy Theatre on June 4, 1947. Unlike later radio, TV, and stage productions, or the 1994 remake starring Richard Attenborough, this *Miracle* was not originally advertised as a Christmas movie. The poster featured Maureen O'Hara and John Payne; though Edmund Gwenn is visible in the background with eight-year-old Natalie Wood, he is not wearing his Santa Claus suit.

In 1947, studio heads had little faith in Christmas movies. Frank Capra's *It's a Wonderful Life* had opened in December 1946, losing money for Liberty Pictures. The film did not become an essential part of the season until the 1960s, when it first appeared on television.

34th Street
Photographed from the Empire State Building

When Christmas arrived in 1947, *A Miracle on 34th Street* was still playing major theatres. Gwenn, who started acting in London's West End Theaters and had been making movies since 1916, won an Oscar and a Golden Globe for his portrayal of Kris Kringle. Writers George Seaton and Valentine Davis also took home Academy Awards for Screenplay and Original Story, though Best Picture went to Elia Kazan's *Gentleman's Agreement*. All the scenes set in R.H. Macy's 34th Street store were shot overnight, when the store was closed.

Rowland Hussey Macy was born on Nantucket in 1822, the son of a merchant ship captain. At fifteen, he joined the crew of the whaling ship *Emily Morgan*. He returned to shore four years later, having worked his way up to Master. For the rest of his life, employees called him "Captain Macy." The backs of his hands were decorated with seaman's tattoos, including the red, five-pointed "lucky star" still featured on Macy's signage and shopping bags.

Macy opened several dry goods stores in Massachusetts before moving to New York in 1858. Though all his earlier stores failed, he tried again at 204 Sixth Avenue. It was a small store, just 17 feet wide and 40 deep. He and his family lived upstairs. On opening day, he took in eleven dollars.

Determined to succeed, Macy traveled to Paris to study the world's first department store, *Le Bon Marche*. He opened a hat department on 14th

Street, and then a toy department next to his original storefront. As the business grew, he moved his family to a house on 12th Street, and then to a larger place on West 49th.

When Macy died in 1877, his store—R.H. Macy & Co.—filled eleven red-brick buildings on Sixth Avenue, between 13th and 14th Streets. His family held onto the business until 1896.

Brothers Nathan and Isadore Straus began working in the store in 1873, when their father, Lazarus, opened a china and glassware department in the basement. They became part owners of Macy's in 1884, sole owners in 1896. Three years earlier, they had also bought Joseph Wechsler's share of Abraham and Wechsler, Brooklyn's biggest department store. The enormous store on Fulton Street operated as Abraham & Straus until 1994, when it became the second-largest Macy's in New York.

The Straus brothers closed the Sixth Avenue store on a Monday: November 3, 1902. Tuesday was Election Day. Macy's employees spent the rest of the week shifting merchandise from the crowded old stores to the company's new palace at 34th and Broadway. The new store contained more than a million square feet of retail space on nine floors, and had taken an entire year to build. The doors opened eight o'clock Saturday morning.

R.H. Macy & Co., main entrance on 34th Street

Isadore and his wife, Ida, died when the *Titanic* sank in April, 1912. Nathan retired two years later and devoted the rest of his life to philanthropy. In 1927, he built a $250,000 Health Center in Jerusalem. The city's *Rehov Straus* (Straus Street) is named in his honor, as is the Israeli city of Netanya, which is on the Mediterranean coast north of Tel Aviv.

Louis Bamberger bought Hill and Cragg, a struggling dry goods store on Market Street in Newark, New Jersey, in 1892. With his sister Caroline and their two business partners, Louis Meyer Frank and Felix Fuld, he started L. Bamberger & Company and turned the store into a moneymaker.

In 1912, Bamberger opened Newark's biggest department store. Designed by Chicago architect Jarvis Hunt, the 14-story building occupied the entire block bounded by Market, Halsey. Washington, and Bank Streets, and had its own telephone exchange (565). The store filled eleven floors, including two basement levels. The tenth floor was a restaurant. When delivery trucks turned in from Washington Street, giant elevators lowered them to loading docks four stories underground. A big, two-faced clock jutting out from the Halsey/Market Street corner quickly became one of Newark's most recognizable landmarks.

For most of its history, Bamberger's competed with two other Newark department stores: Kresge's, which closed in 1964, and Hahne & Company, which lasted until 1986. To draw attention to his store's selection of radios, Bamberger licensed WOR radio in 1922; the studio was on the sixth floor.

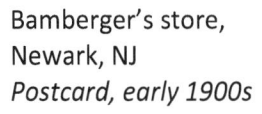

Bamberger's store, Newark, NJ
Postcard, early 1900s

Around the same time, he also launched a Thanksgiving Day Parade. The parade marched up Central Avenue from Bamberger's hometown of South Orange, New Jersey to Market Street, and then turned in at Washington. Santa stepped down from the last float underneath the Washington Street marquee and rode an elevator to the toy department on the eighth floor.

Macy's employees convinced management to sponsor a similar parade on Thanksgiving, 1924. Dressed in fanciful costumes and accompanied by jazz bands and animals borrowed from Central Park Zoo, they marched all the way down from 145th Street in Harlem to the store at 34th. A quarter of a million New Yorkers turned out to watch. The elephants wore blankets decorated with the words MACY'S CHRISTMAS PARADE. Santa rode in on a float and was proclaimed "King of the Kiddies." Posters described it as

A Magnificent Holiday Event: Awe-Inspiring in its Grandeur, Mirth-Provoking in its Comedy, Teeming with a Million Thrills!

There were no live animals in the 1927 parade; apparently some of the "kiddies" were afraid of them. In their place, teams of costumed handlers guided giant animal balloons designed by puppeteer Tony Sarg and made by the Goodyear Tire and Rubber Company. The Toy Soldier was 60 feet tall, 30 wide. The balloons were filled with air and held up on sticks. Puppeteer Bil Baird, who supervised their construction, compared them to "giant upside-down marionettes."

Tony Sarg was born in 1880 in Guatemala, son of the German consul. He moved to England in 1905 and then in 1915 to New York, where he worked as a book illustrator at the iconic Flatiron Building. In the early 1920s, he made several animated cartoons and launched the first of his touring marionette shows, *Rip Van Winkle*. He also designed children's books, toys, department store window displays (including several for Macy's), and marionette productions for the 1933 and 1939 World's Fairs.

Bil Baird, who began working for Sarg in 1928, launched his own puppet company in 1934. Though he created two television shows in the 1950s and made hundreds of commercials and educational films, he is probably best known for *The Lonely Goatherd*, the puppet theater scene in *The Sound of Music* (1965). From 1967 until 1978, Baird ran his own marionette theater on Barrow Street, in New York's West Village.

Named after Charles Goodyear, the inventor of vulcanized rubber, the Goodyear Tire and Rubber Company was founded in Akron, Ohio in 1898. The company launched its first helium-filled advertising blimp, *Pilgrim*, in 1925. In the 1930s, the Goodyear logos on the sides of the blimps were outlined with neon tubes.

Tony Sarg's 120-foot Sea Serpent balloon, photographed on the Nantucket beach in 1937
Nantucket Historical Association

For the 1928 Macy's parade, five of Sarg's balloons were filled with helium. They floated above the city streets on ropes, and their handlers released them at the end of the route. Each balloon had a return address tag attached. The plan was for the giant animals to drift a few days before settling to Earth; anyone who found and returned a balloon would receive a Macy's gift certificate. But the balloons rose too high, too quickly, and burst. For the next few years, the balloons were fitted with valves that allowed the helium to bleed off as the outside pressure dropped. Balloons were last released in 1932, when a small airplane collided with one of them (the pilot survived).

Of course the balloons grew larger and more elaborate over time. For the 1932 parade, Sarg designed a Dachshund that barked and a pig that oinked. The 1937 Pinocchio balloon had a nose 44 feet long; it took 20 handlers just to guide the nose around city corners. The parade's longest balloon was Sarg's 120-foot Nantucket Sea Serpent, the tallest an 80-foot Superman launched in 1980 (an earlier Superman flew down Broadway in 1940).

The tradition of modeling balloons after popular cartoon characters began in 1931 with Felix the Cat, the 1920s star of more than 100 silent cartoons and a syndicated comic strip. Mickey Mouse arrived in 1934, a 40-foot balloon guided by 25 handlers. Snoopy didn't make his Macy's debut until 1968, but the beagle has flown in more parades than any other character (eight different balloons).

A newsreel company filmed the renamed Macy's Thanksgiving Day Parade in 1930, and WOR radio began broadcasting the event in 1938. Macy's canceled the 1942 parade and donated 650 pounds of rubber—including the Sea Serpent—to the war effort. The parade was not held again until 1945, when two million people lined the city's streets to watch. That was also the year the original six mile route was trimmed to two and a half, with the starting point moved down to 77th Street. Audiences around the world saw scenes from the 1946 parade in *A Miracle on 34th Street*, and NBC began its annual television coverage in 1952. The first broadcasts were black and white, and ran only one hour; NBC switched to color in 1960, but did not show the entire three-hour parade until 1969.

The 1946 window displays seen in *A Miracle on 34th Street* were made by the German toy manufacturer Steiff, which produced the first teddy bears in 1902. The animated figures were later sold to FAO Schwarz, and then to a bank in Milwaukee, which still sets them up every Christmas.

Today's balloons are designed and painted at the Macy's Parade Studio in Moonachie, New Jersey and inflated at the intersection of 77th Street and Central Park West, near the American Museum of Natural History. Inflating them all takes ten hours, and the largest balloons require up to 90 handlers; about half of the parade's 4,000 costumed volunteers help guide balloons. Despite annual worries about high winds, the balloons have only been grounded once in the parade's history, in 1971.

Macy's bought Bamberger's in 1929 but operated its old rival as a separate company until 1986, when all the stores were renamed Macy's. Though the Newark location closed in 1991, the building remains. Today it houses tech companies and a handful of stores. The former truck entrance on Washington Street leads to a subterranean parking garage. Until the early 1960s, Macy's ran similar parades in both cities.

After selling the Newark store, Louis and Caroline Bamberger devoted themselves to philanthropy. Caroline gave to a variety of Jewish charities and funded the planting of more than 2,000 cherry trees in Newark's Branch Brook Park.

Louis built permanent homes for the Newark Museum, the Newark YMHA, and the New Jersey Historical Society; he also helped Jewish families escape the Holocaust. Together, the Bamberger's spent a total of $18 million to establish the Institute for Advanced Study in Princeton, New Jersey. When the Institute opened in 1933, its professors included Albert Einstein.

Thanksgiving is not an American invention. In the 1600s, English Puritans did away with most of the old Catholic holidays in favor of occasional Days of Fasting and Days of Thanksgiving. The Pilgrims and other early English settlers brought these traditions to the New World; by some accounts, the first American Day of Thanksgiving was observed in Virginia, in 1607. Fourteen years later, the Pilgrims celebrated their own Day of Thanksgiving in Plymouth Colony, with the Native Americans who helped them survive the Massachusetts winter.

President George Washington declared the first National Day of Thanksgiving on October 3, 1789:

I do recommend and assign Thursday the 26th day of November next to be devoted by the People of these states to the service of that great and glorious Being, who is the beneficent Author of all the good that was, that is, or that will be ... for all the great and various favors which he hath been pleased to confer upon us.

The First Thanksgiving, 1621 (c.1915)
Jean Leon Gerome Ferris; from his series of historical paintings, *The Pageant of a Nation*

The holiday has been celebrated every November since 1863, when President Abraham Lincoln announced another National Day of Thanksgiving. Until 1939, Thanksgiving was always celebrated on the last Thursday of November.

President Franklin Roosevelt moved Thanksgiving to the fourth Thursday in November in 1939. His reason? November had five Thursdays that year, and an extra week of Christmas shopping would be good for the economy (in those days, stores did not set up Christmas displays until the day after Thanksgiving). Though Republicans labeled the new date "Franksgiving," Roosevelt considered the experiment a success. Because the next two Novembers had only four Thursdays each, he announced in 1940 and again in 1941 that

Thanksgiving would fall on the third. Some states went along with him, others didn't. In 1942, both houses of Congress passed a resolution returning Thanksgiving to the fourth Thursday in November. FDR signed, and the date hasn't changed since... no matter how many retail chains set up their Christmas displays in October.

Antique Thanksgiving Postcard

New Year, New York

The traditional end of the Christmas season is January 6: Epiphany, when the wise men arrived at Bethlehem with their gifts of gold, frankincense, and myrrh. But in the fast-paced modern world, school and work usually resume right after New Year's Day.

In the Western world, the years have started on January 1 since 153 BC (before that, the Roman year started in March). The ancient Babylonian year also started in March, the Chinese and Vietnamese years between January 21 and February 21, and the Aztec and Mayan calendars on February 23. *Rosh Hashanah*, Hebrew for "Head of the Year," usually falls between the middle and end of September. Because Islamic nations still use a lunar calendar, the first day of their first month shifts about in relation to the western calendar—September 12 in 2018, August 20 in 2020.

The Roman calendar was revised in 46 BC, during the reign of Julius Caesar. The resulting Julian calendar was used throughout Europe until October 1852, when Pope Gregory XIII introduced a more accurate one. Because the Julian calendar had fallen out of sync with the annual solstices, Catholic nations had an unusual October that year. October 4 was a Thursday; Friday was the 15th.

The British Empire—including the American colonies—did not adopt this Gregorian calendar until 1752. (They called it the "New Style" calendar, because good Anglicans would not use a calendar named for a Pope!) Meanwhile, some Eastern Orthodox churches still follow the old Julian calendar.

Two of the four New Testament Gospels describe the birth of Jesus. In Matthew 1:18, "Mary ... was found with child of the Holy Ghost." An angel tells Joseph "she shall bring forth a son, and thou shalt call his name JESUS: for he shall save his people from their sins." In Luke 1:26, the angel Gabriel appears to Mary, to say she "hast found favour with God," and "shalt conceive in thy womb, and bring forth a son, and shalt call his name JESUS. He shall be great, and shall be called the Son of the Highest."

Annunciation (1475)
Leonardo da Vinci painting of Gabriel and Mary
Uffizi Gallery, Florence, Italy

Both writers tell us Jesus was born in Bethlehem, Luke adding that "she laid him in a manger; because there was no room for them in the inn." But neither tells us the date—or even the month—in which the miracle occurred. For several centuries, different churches celebrated the Nativity on different dates.

In 325 AD, Roman Emperor Constantine the Great announced a Christmas feast on the winter solstice—December 25 on the Julian calendar. Though Constantine did not officially convert to Christianity until the day he died, he ended the Roman persecution of Christians in 313. A dozen years later, he arranged the First Council of Nicaea, where hundreds of bishops gathered to debate what it meant to be a Christian (Nicholas of Myra may have attended). The summary they composed, called the Nicene Creed, is still read in churches today, affirming belief in the Divine Trinity of

Father, Son, and Holy Spirit. Constantine also had the first Church of the Holy Sepulchre built on what is believed to be the site of Christ's crucifixion and burial. Burned by the Persians in 614, the church was first rebuilt by the Crusaders in the 1100s.

Pope Julius I was elected in 337, the year Constantine died. Around 345, he made December 25 the official date of Jesus' birth. By the Middle Ages, Christmas had mostly replaced Europe's old pagan winter festivals.

Only Matthew mentions the coming of "wise men from the east to Jerusalem." He tells us almost nothing about them. The idea that there were three of them is based on the number of gifts he mentions, the tradition that they were Kings on Old Testament prophecies; Psalm 72 promises that "all kings shall fall down before him; all nations shall serve him." Historians believe they were probably Zoroastrian astrologer priests from Persia.

Though modern Nativity scenes (including Radio City Music Hall's "Living Nativity") include both shepherds and wise men or kings, Christian tradition does not place them there at the same time. Because they came from much farther away, the wise men are believed to have arrived on January 6, rather than Christmas Day. The day is called Epiphany: the moment when the Son of God was first revealed to the outside world.

The Star of Bethlehem (1890)
Edward Burne-Jones
Birmingham Museum, England

Spanish nations celebrate the Feast of the Three Kings on January 6; children leave snacks for the visitors on the night of January 5 and receive gifts in the morning. In other traditions, January 6 is celebrated as the anniversary of Jesus' baptism, or of his first miracle (turning water to wine, during a wedding in Cana).

In Elizabethan England, January 5 was celebrated as "Twelfth Night," a rowdy carnival. William Shakespeare's *Twelfth Night*, first presented at the end of the Christmas season in 1602, is a comedy of mistaken identities.

Though we do not celebrate Twelfth Night in the United States, we do sing about *The Twelve Days of Christmas*—the twelve days starting on December

25 and ending January 5.The lyric first appeared in the 1780 children's book *Mirth Without Mischief* as a sort of memory game, each verse adding another nonsensical gift to remember. Frederic Austin, an English opera singer and theatrical composer, set the words to music in 1909.

In nineteenth century New York, crowds gathered around Broadway's Trinity Church every December 31 for the midnight ringing of the bells. Publisher Adolph Ochs decided to move the celebration a few miles uptown in 1904.

Born in Cincinnati in 1858, Ochs bought his first newspaper, the *Chattanooga Times Free Press*, when he was nineteen. In 1896, he bought the *New York Times*. Because the paper had only 9,000 subscribers, he dropped the daily price from three cents to a penny and promised "All the News That's Fit to Print." By the 1920s, the *Times* had 780,000 subscribers.

In 1904, Ochs built the paper a new home: a 25-story skyscraper at Longacre Square, where Broadway crossed Seventh Avenue at 42nd Street. Counting the 70-foot flagpole, the tower was 363 feet high—second tallest in the city. (The Park Row Building, completed in 1899, is 390 feet tall; it overlooks the southern tip of City Hall Park, a block away from the original *Times* building.) Though the *Times*' reputation was built on objectivity, the editors were not above including four basement levels to increase their tower's height.

Trinity Church (1846)
Photographed from Wall Street

One Times Square / *New York Times* Building (1904)
Photographed by Irving Underhill in 1905

New York's first subway also opened in 1904. Ochs convinced the city to build a station under his building, and talked Mayor George McClellan, Jr. into renaming the busy intersection "Times Square." Merchants had nicknamed it Longacre a few decades earlier, borrowing the name from a London street known for its carriage shops.

On December 31, 1904, Ochs set up a street fair around his new building. As midnight approached, he shot fireworks from the top of the tower. Midnight was announced with what the *Times* itself described as a "dynamite bomb." By some accounts, the festivities were heard all the way up in Croton-on-Hudson, 30 miles to the north. The *Times* repeated the show in 1905 and 1906, crowds of 200,000 braving the winter cold and the rain of hot ash from the explosives.

In 1907, the city police refused to issue a fireworks permit.

Ochs quickly found another way to draw a crowd on New Year's Eve. Every day, people on lower Broadway paused to look up at the top of the ten-story Western Union Building. At precisely noon, a metal ball three and a half feet in diameter began sliding down the flagpole to the roof. Many New Yorkers set their watches by it.

The first "time ball" was set up in England in 1833, for the benefit of ships' captains in Portsmouth Harbor. The United States Naval Observatory built one in Washington, D.C. in 1845, and they became common sights in town squares after the Civil War.

On the evening of December 31, 1907, workers used ropes and pulleys to raise a five-foot ball to the top of the *Times* Building's flagpole. Designed by Walter Palmer, the building's chief electrician, the ball contained 100 electric lights. Built of wood and iron by Jacob Starr, an eighteen-year-old Russian immigrant, it weighed 700 pounds.

New Year Postcard, 1908

Workers began lowering the ball at 11:59. When it touched the roof at midnight, an electric sign flashed on at the top of the tower: "1908." Smaller versions of the sign glowed on the top hats worn by all the waiters in the fancy Times Square restaurants.

Starr soon found work with the Strauss Sign Company, designing theater marquees and other large advertisements. He started his own neon sign company, Artkraft, in the 1920s, and then merged with Strauss Sign in 1931 to form Artkraft Strauss. By the 1950s, Artkraft Strauss was building and operating most of the lighted signs in Times Square (Starr called the largest signs "spectaculars"). For most of the twentieth century, the company also managed the annual New Year's Eve Ball Drop.

The original wood and iron ball was replaced in 1920 with a 400-pound wrought iron ball, and then in 1955 with a lighter aluminum ball. The only years the ball was not dropped were 1942 and 1943. During the wartime blackouts, midnight was greeted with a moment of silence, followed by the ringing of the Trinity Church bells, the sound broadcast from downtown to speaker trucks.

Though the *New York Times* owned the tower until 1961, the paper moved to more spacious quarters on 43rd Street in 1913 (the *Times* moved again in 2007, to a new 52-story skyscraper on Eighth Avenue, across from the Port Authority Bus Terminal). In 1928, the paper's owners installed the Motograph News Bulletin—the first lighted news "zipper"—on the tower. The letters, which rolled around a motorized track, were made up of almost 15,000 lightbulbs. Millions gathered around the building on the evening of August 14, 1945, waiting for the news from Washington, D.C. At 7:03, a five-word headline began scrolling: "Official—Truman announces Japanese surrender." The motorized zipper was replaced in 1995 with an electronic version run by Dow Jones.

The developer who bought the building in 1961 removed its granite and terra cotta decorations and refaced it with marble. In the 1980s, when Times Square was overrun with crime and vice, the city government considered condemning and demolishing the mostly empty tower. Audiences for the ball drop had plummeted, from more than a million people a year in the 1950s to just 50,000 in the late 1970s. (Ironically, the 1980s ball was decorated as a giant red Big Apple for the city's "I Love New York" advertising campaign.)

Lehman Brothers bought the building in 1995, left the office floors empty, and covered the outside walls with a grid for lighted signs. Recent plans for the tower include opening a Times Square Museum inside, with a public observation deck on the 18th floor.

CBS began televising the ball drop in the 1950s, as part of an annual broadcast featuring "Mr. New Year's Eve," bandleader Guy Lombardo. At midnight in the Waldorf-Astoria ballroom, his Royal Canadians played their signature tune, the old Scottish ballad *Auld Lang Syne*.

In 1972, *American Bandstand* host Dick Clark convinced rival network NBC to program something for younger viewers: *Three Dog Night's New Year's Rockin' Eve*. In between taped musical performances, Clark reported on the festivities at

Times Square. The following year, comedian George Carlin hosted. Clark took over hosting duties when the show moved to ABC in 1974; headliners that night included Chicago, the Doobie Brothers, Herbie Hancock, Olivia Newton-John, and the Beach Boys. *Dick Clark's New Year's Rockin' Eve* has aired every year since, Clark hosting until he suffered a stroke in December, 2004. Since Ryan Seacrest began hosting in 2006, the show has included live musical performances from Times Square.

The modern ball is twelve feet in diameter, covered with colored panels of Waterford Crystal, and filled with more than 32,000 LED lamps. Since 2009, it has remained in place on top of the tower, easily visible to the passing crowds. At 6 p.m. each New Year's Eve, it is raised to the top of the flagpole. As many as two million people gather every December 31 to watch it drop.

Antique Happy New Year card

Christmas Unwrapped: A Stocking Full of Trivia

We've all seen the abbreviation "Xmas" on advertisements and signs; you may even find it on Christmas cards or decorations. Some find it offensive, and say that writing "Xmas" is "removing Christ from Christmas." But the abbreviation is neither a recent invention, nor a secular one.

The first two letters of the Greek word *Christos* are **X** and **P**, pronounced *Chi* and *Rho*. On Orthodox icons, they are often combined into a single symbol, the *Chi-Rho*. Sometimes, just the cross-like **X** is used to represent Christ.

Johann Gutenberg perfected his printing press in the 1450s. Setting the type by hand was time-consuming, and parchment was expensive. To save time and money, the Greek **X** often replaced the word "Christ" in Church documents, and "Christmas" was shortened to "Xmas." In the nineteenth century, Lord Byron, Samuel Coleridge, and Lewis Carroll all used the abbreviation, and newspapers sometimes shortened "Christian" to "Xian" and "Christianity" to "Xianity." Readers understood that the entire word was meant to be pronounced—"Christmas," not "exmas."

Inset: *Chi* and *Rho* symbols from the first chapter of Matthew, in the 9th-century Book of Kells.
Trinity College Library Dublin, Ireland

Glassblowers Hans Greiner and Christoph Muller founded the town of Lauscha, Germany in 1597. More than 400 years later, glassmaking is still the town's biggest industry.

In the 1800s, the town's cottage manufacturers turned out a wide variety of products, including colored glass beads, marbles, and artificial eyes. By

135

mid-century, some were also blowing tubes of heated glass into wooden molds to make Christmas tree ornaments. The first Lauscha ornaments were simple replicas of the fruits and nuts German families had been decorating their trees with for generations. More elaborate designs, blown in ceramic molds, appeared in the 1870s.

Frank Winfield Woolworth opened his first store in Utica, New York in 1878. Everything sold for the same price: five cents (about $1.30 in 2017). Though the store failed after only a few months, he tried again the following year, opening his first Woolworth's Five and Ten Cent Store in Lancaster, Pennsylvania. When he died in 1919, Woolworth had more than a thousand stores.

In the 1880s, Woolworth began taking annual trips to Europe, looking for low-priced goods to import. One of his first discoveries was Lauscha glass ornaments; by 1900, he was buying 200,000 a year, mostly simple red glass balls.

Woolworth was also one of the first employers to pay Christmas bonuses, up to $25 for employees who had been with the company five years or more. (Doesn't sound like much. But adjusted for inflation, a $25 bonus in 1910 would be worth $665 in 2018!)

The Corning Glass Company began making light bulbs for Edison in 1879. Bulbs accounted for half of the company's business in 1908, and by the 1920s, Corning had machines that could turn out 400,000 bulbs a day.

German immigrant Max Eckardt founded the Shiny Bright Company in 1937. At his factories in West New York and North Bergen, New Jersey, workers hand-painted glass baubles and packed them in distinctive cardboard boxes. Eckardt bought the balls in quantity from Corning Glass, which made them with machines originally developed to mass-produce light bulbs. The inexpensive ornament sets, sold through department stores and mail order catalogs, dominated the American market until the 1960s.

The tradition of decorating Christmas trees with candy canes goes back to at least the late 1800s, though they may have been invented as early as 1670. According to one popular story, the choirmaster at Germany's Cologne Cathedral ordered the sweets from a local confectioner to keep children quiet during long services; the hooked shape was meant to remind them of shepherds' crooks.

Peppermint flavor was first added in the early 1900s, but candy canes remained pure white until the 1920s. Bob McCormack, who manufactured sweets in Albany, Georgia, was the first to find a practical way of adding colored stripes. But even in his factory, workers had to bend the canes by hand. A lot of canes were broken before McCormack's brother-in-law, Gregory Harding Keller, invented an automatic bending machine in 1957.

Henry Cole worked on reforming the British mail system in the 1830s, serving on the committees that created the Penny Post and the world's first postage stamp. He helped organize the Great Exhibition of 1851, which was held inside an enormous iron and glass "Crystal Palace" in London's Hyde Park, and was one of the founders of the Victoria and Albert Museum. He even wrote educational children's books under a pseudonym.

But in 1843, Cole had a problem: he was too busy to write Christmas letters to his many friends. Instead, he hired artist John Callcott Horsley to design the world's first Christmas card: a picture of a family enjoying a holiday meal, a banner with the words "Merry Christmas and a Happy New Year to You," and blank spaces for the addressee's name and Cole's signature. Cole ordered a thousand copies from a London printer, filled in the blanks, and mailed them out for a penny apiece. Cole began selling lithographed cards the following season, and by the 1850s, printed cards were available throughout Europe.

Artist and publisher Louis Prang discovered Christmas cards while visiting Germany in the 1860s. After studying the latest innovations in chromolithography (an early form of color printing), Prang returned to Massachusetts, where he began publishing high-quality reproductions of famous paintings. Some required up to 40 hand-carved stone plates, one for each color.

Henry Cole's Christmas card (1843)
Artist: John Callcott Horsely.

Prang also published art books, both history and technique, and sold a variety of artists' supplies, including the first nontoxic watercolors for children. He printed his first pocket-sized Christmas cards in 1875. By 1881 he was selling five million a year—and they weren't cheap. Some sold in sets of 12 for three dollars. Larger cards, six inches by eight, sold for up to 75 cents each, or $1.25 with a silk fringe.

In the spring of 1880, Prang offered prizes ranging from $200 to $1000 (about $25,000 in 2018) for Christmas card designs. Out of 800 submissions, his judges awarded the top prize to a picture of five children singing carols. Though he limited the 1881 contest to American artists, the company received 1500 submissions. Prang discontinued the contest after the 1884 season, and stopped printing cards in the 1890s, when cheap imports flooded the market.

During the 1880s, Prang also published cards for Easter and Valentine's Day. The United States Post Office honored him in 1975, with a stamp based on one of his earliest cards.

Prang's Christmas Cards from 1876 and 1884.
Verse from the 1884 card:
On the Yule-log here I ride. With it set the fire ablaze. And I wish to you beside Many Merry Christmas days.

Prang's Christmas Cards (1881 advertisement)

Pyotr Tchaikovsky's three-hour ballet *The Sleeping Beauty* debuted at Saint Petersburg's Imperial Mariinsky Theatre in 1890. For the 1892 season, the directors asked him to write a double bill, consisting of an opera and a ballet. Choreographer Marius Petipa suggested basing the ballet on *The Nutcracker*, Alexander Dumas' 1859 adaptation of E.T.A. Hoffman's 1816 fantasy novel *The Nutcracker and the Mouse King*.

Tchaikovsky didn't like the story, and when *The Nutcracker* debuted in December 1892, along with his one act opera *Iolanta*, it was not well received. For many years, the 20-minute *Nutcracker Suite* Tchaikovsky assembled from the main themes—the *Dance of the Sugar Plum Fairy*, *Waltz of the Flowers*, and the Russian, Arabian, and Chinese dances—was more popular than the ballet. (In 1940, Walt Disney included an abbreviated version of the *Suite* in *Fantasia*. In place of the ballet's characters, his animators filled movie screens with dancing fish, flowers, leaves, and mushrooms.) The complete ballet was not performed outside of Russia until 1934.

George Balanchine moved from Saint Petersburg to New York in 1933. While working as a Broadway choreographer, he cofounded the School of American Ballet and then the New York City Ballet. He first staged *The Nutcracker* in December 1954, one of the first American productions to use Tchaikovsky's complete score. Today *The Nutcracker* is an annual tradition for many

American ballet companies, including the New York City Ballet, which still presents Balanchine's version every Christmas.

English pastor Isaac Watts based his 1719 hymn *Joy to the World* on Psalm 98, which calls for the faithful to:

> *Make a joyful noise unto the LORD, all the earth;*
> *Make a loud noise, and rejoice, and sing praise.*
> *Sing unto the LORD with the harp;*
> *with the harp, and the voice of a psalm.*
> *With trumpets and sound of cornet*
> *make a joyful noise before the LORD, the King.*

American composer Lowell Mason published *Occasional Psalms and Hymn Tunes* in 1836. Determined to introduce Americans to the European classics, he based the tune *Antioch* on two melodies from George Frederick Handel's 1741 oratorio *Messiah*. (Best known for its rousing "Hallelujah Chorus," *Messiah* was originally performed at Easter, rather than Christmas.) In the United States, *Antioch* has been paired with Watts' hymn since the 1840s.

Mason wrote the music for more than 1600 hymns. In the 1830s, he also composed a melody for a poem by *Godey's Lady's Book* editor Sarah Josepha Hale: *Mary Had a Little Lamb* (the verses were first published in her 1830 book *Poems for Our Children*, as *Mary's Lamb*.)

The Road,—Winter (1853)
Lithograph, Currier & Ives

One of the most popular songs of the Christmas season never mentions the holiday, and may originally have been performed at a Thanksgiving celebration. Two different towns claim to be the birthplace of *The One Horse Open Sleigh*: Medford Massachusetts, where composer James Lord Pierpont was born, and Savannah, Georgia, where he directed the choir at the Unitarian Church in the 1850s. Pierpont copyrighted the song in 1857 and published it two years later as *Jingle Bells, or the One Horse Open Sleigh*.

One popular story says the song was first performed by a Sunday School choir. Many historians consider this unlikely; for the 1850s, *Jingle Bells* was actually a rather risqué story of courting, the nineteenth century equivalent of early rock'n'roll car songs:

A day or two ago, I thought I'd take a ride
And soon Miss Fanny Bright
was seated by my side
The horse was lean and lank,
misfortune seemed his lot
He got into a drifted bank
and then we got upsot

And from the fourth verse:

Now the ground is white,
go it while you're young;
Take the girls tonight,
and sing this sleighing song.
Just get a bobtailed bay,
two forty as his speed
Hitch him to an open sleigh
and crack! You'll take the lead

Jingle Bells is not only one of the most recorded Christmas songs of all time—it may also have been the first. The Edison Company released a wax cylinder recording of *Jingle Bells* in 1889: a man named Will Lyle singing and accompanying himself on banjo. This recording is believed to be lost. But online, you can listen to an 1898 wax recording by the Edison Male Quartet. *Jingle Bells* is one of several popular songs included in their comedic *Sleigh Ride Party*. After parting with Edison in the early 1900s, the group scored several hits as the Hayden Quartet, including *In the Good Old Summer Time* and *Take Me Out to the Ball Game*.

James Pierpont's nephew, John Pierpont Morgan, was once America's most powerful banker; his name and legacy live on as part of JP Morgan Chase.

Irving Berlin did not write *White Christmas* for the 1954 movie of that name. The song first appeared in the 1942 Paramount feature *Holiday Inn*, starring Bing Crosby and Fred Astaire. Berlin wrote a dozen songs for the movie, including *White Christmas*; he also reused *Easter Parade*, which he had written for the 1933 Broadway review *As Thousands Cheer*. (*Easter Parade* would make its third appearance in 1948, as the title song of an MGM musical starring Astaire and Judy Garland.)

Holiday Inn premiered at New York's Paramount Theatre in August, 1942. Bing Crosby's recording of *White Christmas* topped the charts that October, and remained at #1 for eleven weeks. At the 1943 Academy Awards, *White Christmas* won Best Original Song. Berlin was also nominated for Best Original Story, losing to the British war film *The Invaders* (released in the United States as *49th Parallel*).

Over the years, Crosby's *White Christmas* has sold an estimated 100 million copies; it was considered the bestselling single of all time until 1997, when Elton John reworked *Candle in the Wind* as *Goodbye England's Rose*, a tribute to the late Princess Diana.

Due to the song's ongoing popularity, Paramount built another movie around it in 1954, also starring Bing Crosby, this time with Danny Kaye and Rosemary Clooney. Parts of *White Christmas* were filmed at the same Connecticut hotel featured in *Holiday Inn*. Released in October, it was the first movie shot in VistaVision—Paramount's new 70mm widescreen format—and the year's top moneymaker. Irving Berlin wrote all the songs, including *Count Your Blessings (Instead of Sheep)*, which was nominated for Best Original Song (the statuette went to *Three Coins in the Fountain*, by Jule Styne and Sammy Cahn).

In July 1945, lyricist Robert Wells tried to take his mind off the heat by rhyming a few lines about fond winter memories—Jack Frost, Christmas choirs, and roasting chestnuts. Jazz singer and pianist Mel Torme recognized the beginning of a hit song when he saw one, and quickly worked out a melody; in less than an hour, he and Wells had completed the words and music.

Nat "King" Cole first recorded *The Christmas Song* with his trio—Cole on piano and vocals, Oscar Moore on guitar, and Wesley Prince on bass—in 1946. He rerecorded the song later that year with a small string section, and then in 1953 with a full orchestra conducted by Nelson Riddle. What you usually hear on the radio is the stereo version he cut in 1961.

Fresh out of the United States Army, Leroy Anderson spent the summer of 1946 at his mother-in-law's cottage in Woodbury, Connecticut. Like Torme and Wells, Anderson found himself thinking about winter during a July heatwave and starting composing a sleigh riding tune. He completed *Sleigh Ride* in February 1948. Conductor Arthur Fiedler recorded it with the Boston Pops Orchestra the following year.

Like most of Anderson's pieces, *Sleigh Ride* was originally an instrumental. The Andrews Sisters cut the first vocal version in 1950, after songwriter Mitchell Parrish added lyrics. Parrish also wrote the words to Hoagy Carmichael's *Stardust* and Duke Ellington's *Sophisticated Lady*, among many others. Because *Sleigh Ride* is performed so often at Christmastime, some singers change the lyric's "Birthday Party" to "Christmas Party."

At one point in the song, Parrish compares the ride to a Currier and Ives "picture print."

Artist and lithographer Nathaniel Currier began publishing inexpensive prints in the 1830s. At first, only the underlying black and white drawings were printed; his staff added the colors by hand. Later on, Currier used multiple plates to print full-color images. His early successes included disaster scenes, such as the fire that devastated New York's business district in December, 1835.

Currier hired James Merritt Ives as a bookkeeper, promoted him to general manager, and then made him a full partner in 1857. Though not an artist himself, Ives had an eye for talent and a clear sense of what the public would buy. By 1866, Currier & Ives filled three floors of a commercial building on Spruce Street in lower Manhattan.

At their height, Currier & Ives released two or three new images every week, everything from sentimental scenes to political satire. You could buy prints from bookstores, pushcart vendors, and mail order catalogs. Postcard-sized prints sold for as little as five cents, framable wall prints for a few dollars.

Many of the company's artists specialized. Frances Palmer drew American landscapes, Arthur Tait did sports pictures. George H. Durrie was known the for sort of rural winter scenes Parrish had in mind when he wrote *Sleigh Ride*.

Currier died in 1888, Ives in 1895. Though the company was shuttered in 1907, their work lives on in books, on Christmas cards, and as fine art prints. Especially popular and collectible are their many winter pictures—rural scenes, Central Park ice skaters, and—of course—sleigh rides.

Currier & Ives

American Homestead Winter (1868)

Winter in the Country – The Old Grist Mill (1864)

Winter Scenes

Central-Park, Winter – The Skating Pond (1862)

Winter in the Country – A Cold Morning (1864)

The Sun Building Clock on the corner of Broadway and Chambers Street is decorated with the newspaper's motto: "The Sun, it shines for all."

The most "New York" of all Christmas stories didn't actually happen during the Christmas season. It was late summer, 1897, when eight-year-old Laura Virginia O'Hanlon wrote a short letter to *The Sun*, one of the city's most popular dailies.

Dear Editor –
I am 8 years old. Some of my little friends say there is no Santa Claus. Papa says "if you see it in the Sun It's so." Please tell me the truth, is there a Santa Claus?

The paper finally printed a response on Tuesday, September 21, on the editorial page. "Virginia," wrote Francis Church, "your little friends are wrong. They have been affected by the skepticism of a skeptical age."

Yes, Virginia, there is a Santa Claus. He exists as certainly as love and generosity and devotion exist ... Alas! How dreary would be the world if there were no Santa Claus! It would be as dreary as if there were no Virginias ...

Not believe in Santa Claus! You might as well not believe in fairies! You might get your papa to hire men to watch in all the chimneys on Christmas Eve to catch Santa Claus, but even if they did not see Santa Claus coming down, what would that prove? Nobody sees Santa Claus, but that is no sign that there is no Santa Claus ...

No Santa Claus! Thank God! He lives, and he lives forever. A thousand years from now, Virginia, nay, ten times ten thousand years from now, he will continue to make glad the heart of childhood.

Like all the paper's editorials, the reply was unsigned; Church was not identified as the author until after he died in 1906. From the 1920s until the paper ceased publication in 1950, *The Sun* reprinted O'Hanlon's letter and Church's response every December.

Virginia O'Hanlon devoted her life to education, working as an elementary school teacher and principal, earning a Master's degree from Columbia and a doctorate from Fordham. She retired in 1959 and died in 1971, at the age of 81. In 2009, a private elementary school moved into 115 West 95th Street, the 1880s brownstone where she wrote her famous letter; that same year, The Studio School established the Virginia O'Hanlon Scholarship Fund.

IN THE WORDS OF SAINT NICHOLAS
(as recorded by Clement Clarke Moore):

Happy Christmas to all, and to all a good night!

Mini Lights
Photographed by the author

About the Author

KEVIN WOYCE is an author, photographer, and lecturer, specializing in regional American History. A lifelong resident of the Garden State, he grew up in East Rutherford—the eldest of 15 siblings—and now lives in Lyndhurst. He speaks frequently throughout New Jersey and southern New York, on a variety of historical topics.

Website: Kevinwoyce.com
Facebook: Kevin Woyce Author

Books:
Jersey Shore History & Facts
Hudson River Lighthouses
Niagara: The Falls and the River
Liberty
New Jersey State Parks: History & Facts
Lighthouses: Connecticut & Block Island
Powerful PowerPoint
California Visions: Photographs
Bridges: Photographs

Selected Bibliography

Armstrong, Nancy. *The Rockefeller Center Christmas Tree.* Kennebunkport: Cider Mill Press, 2009.

Burns, Ric. *New York: An Illustrated History.* New York: Alfred A. Knopf, 1999.

Collins, Ace. *Stories Behind the Great Traditions of Christmas.* Grand Rapids: Zondervan, 2003.

Dickens, Charles. *A Christmas Carol.* 1843.

Dickens, Charles. *American Notes.* 1843.

Dickens, Charles. *The Pickwick Papers.* 1836.

Federal Writer' Project. *New York City Guide.* New York: Random House, 1939.

Hoffman, Charles (ed.). *The New-York Book of Poetry.* 1837.

Holy Bible (King James Version).

Hungerford, Edward. *The Romance of a Great Store.* New York: Robert M. McBridge & Company, 1922.

Irving, Washington. *The History of New York.* 1809.

Irving, Washington. *The Sketch Book.* 1819-20.

Irving, Washington. *Salmagundi.* 1807-08.

Lester, Meera. *Why Does Santa Wear Red?* Avon: F&W Publications, Inc., 2007.

May, Robert. *Rudolph the Red-Nosed Reindeer.* Chicago: Montgomery Ward & Co., 1939.

Moore, Charles. *A Visit from St. Nicholas.* 1822.

Nast, Thomas. *Thomas Nast's Christmas Drawings for the Human Race.* New York: Harper & Brothers, 1890.

Okrent, Daniel. *Great Fortune: The Epic of Rockefeller Center.* New York: Viking, 2003.

Stansbury, Arthur. *The Children's Friend.* 1821.

Selected Online Sources:

archive.org
Best-norman-rockwell-art
biography.com
birminghammuseums.org.uk
Britannica.com
Coca-colacompany.com
Corning.com
Daytoninmanhattan.blogspot
dickensletters.com
Edison.rutgers.edu
godeysladysbook.com
History.com
Hymnsandcarolsofchristmas
Imdb.com
Macys.com
leroyandersonfoundation.org
Newarkmemories.com
Nypl.org/blog
Nytimes.com
Oldchristmastreelights.com
Performingsongwriter.com
rockefellercenter.com
rockettes.com
stnicholascenter.org
timessquarenyc.org
victorianweb.org
whitehousehistory.org
Whychristmas.com

Made in the USA
Lexington, KY
15 November 2019